Peninsulas in Repose

The Necks of Virginia's Eastern Shore

Curtis J. Badger

Copyright © 2023 by Curtis J. Badger

All rights reserved.

ISBN 978-1-62806-387-5 (print | paperback)

Library of Congress Control Number 2023917067

Published by Salt Water Media
29 Broad Street, Suite 104
Berlin, MD 21811
www.saltwatermedia.com

Cover image: This map of the Eastern Shore was made around 1720 by Johann Baptist Homann (1663-1724) and was included in an atlas published in Nurenberg, Germany in 1788. It shows three counties – Northampton, Accomac, and Arcadia – and many of the waterways are shown, with spellings used in the day. Creeks include Muddy, Guilford, Chesconnessex, Kings, and Occohannock. Barrier islands include Metompkin, Machipongo, Mockhorn, and Smiths. Fisherman Island had not yet formed when this map was made. Map courtesy of the David Rumsey Map Collection, David Rumsey Map Center, Stanford University Libraries.

Interior images are courtesy of the author Curtis Badger, the public domain, and Bill Nelson Cartography, Gordon Campbell, and Cal H. Bundick. The maps are from the David Rumsey Map Collection, David Rumsey Map Center, Stanford Libraries.

Portions of the chapter "Peninsulas in Repose" appeared in the book *Wilderness Regained*

To Tom and Scarlett
With Love

Other Books by Curtis J. Badger

Salt Tide – Cycles and Currents of Life Along the Coast

Bellevue Farm – Exploring Virginia's Coastal Countryside

The Wild Coast – Swamps and Wetlands of the Mid-Atlantic Coast

Virginia's Wild Side – 50 Outdoor Adventures
from the Mountains to the Ocean

A Natural History of Quiet Waters

Exploring Delmarva

A Culinary History of Delmarva

Wilderness Regained – The Story of the Virginia Barrier Islands

Books for Young Readers

Nathan Cobb's Island

Hog Island

Contents

Acknowledgements i

Introduction iii

Peninsulas in Repose 1

Old Plantation and a White Man Called Savage 13

English Customs Become American Ways 20

The Upshurs and a Life of Service 34

Planters, Mariners, and Merchants 54

Sex and Violence in Gargathy Neck 69

When the Waterway Was Our Highway 79

Margaret Twyford's Occohannock Neck 88

Sometimes the Quiet Ones Tell the Best Stories 101

The Bennett Brothers and the Blockade Runners of Hacks Neck ... 113

Savage Neck Dunes 131

Following the Water on Joynes Neck 137

Bowman's Folly and Cropper's Revenge 144

Three Peninsulas at Attention 148

Coda 156

Glossary 159

Bibliography 162

Index 167

Acknowledgements

This book is the result of a great deal of teamwork. It would not have been possible without the generous support of many friends. First of all, I have to thank my friends who are historians and genealogists, who graciously shared their knowledge and provided valuable advice. These include Brooks Miles Barnes, Dennis Custis, Jenean Hall, and M.K. Miles. I should also mention those who came before us, people like Susie May Ames, James E. Mears, John A. Upshur, Thomas T. Upshur, Ralph T. Whitelaw, Jennings C. Wise, and John Sergeant Wise, who have made immense contributions to the body of knowledge of Eastern Shore history.

I am not a historian. I majored in English in college and then entered an MFA Writing program at Warren Wilson College in Swannanoa, North Carolina. So my background is in writing stories, and I love history because that is where so many good stories are. For people who think history is boring, I urge you to read the stories of high drama in Gargathy Neck, night time raids in Joynes Neck, the mysterious creature of Craddock Neck, or the blockade runners of Hacks Neck. And then consider the contributions families such as the Upshurs, Parramores, and Wises have made to the Eastern Shore and the nation. These are the families that populated our necks of the woods generations ago, and whose descendants are still among us.

I want to thank Bill Sterling and his Craddock Neck family and friends, Gayle Shaw and George Boggs, Kim Miles, Rod and Martha Hennessey of Bells Neck, Bill Nelson, who supplied the excellent maps, the very talented photographer Gordon Campbell, who has captured the spirit of the Eastern Shore in his stunning aerial images.

I especially need to thank my wife Lynn who helped with this project in so many ways. She is an excellent editor and organizer and it was she who created the index for this book. I greatly appreciate her patience for the many times my thoughts drifted away from family matters to dwell in places with people who populated our homeland many generations ago.

I also need to thank my daughter-in-law, Scarlett Philibosian, who was the inspiration for this book. Scarlett is a collector of old, archaic words that are no longer in modern use, but which stir the imagination. One such is demi-isle, which was used to describe a peninsula before peninsula became part of the English language. Of course, we live on a peninsula, a demi-isle, and our peninsula is made up of dozens of other demi-isles, which have become known as necks. So, armed with that bit of information, I began investigating the role necks, or demi-isles, played in our past. I have to say I was amazed at what I found.

I hope you will enjoy reading these accounts as much as I enjoyed discovering and sharing them.

Introduction

This book is going to require a bit of imagination on the part of the reader. We are going to travel back to the fall of 1883 and see what the Eastern Shore was like in those days. The railroad came through in 1884, creating a seismic change in the lifestyle and landscape of the peninsula. In this book we are going to do away with the railroad and everything that came with it, all the stations and the towns that grew up around them, all the infrastructure, even U.S. Route 13, that great ribbon of asphalt that ran cheek by jowl with much of the railway from the late 1920s on. All of it goes. When we finish, we will see the Eastern Shore as it was before the railroad and Route 13 began moving people and cargo up and down the coast in a feverish stream.

We will start with Cape Charles City. A city no more, it reverts to a swampy spot in a neck of land between Old Plantation and Kings Creek. The real Cape Charles returns to its maritime duty, demarking the northern entrance to the Chesapeake Bay, stationed across the mouth of the estuary from its cousin, Cape Henry.

They have saved us from removing the railroad itself, most of it having been pried up to make way for a biking and hiking trail. But we will remove the towns the railroad created. Cheriton becomes Sunnyside once again, Eastville loses its station, Nassawadox becomes Nussawattox once more and is returned to the horns of Hungars Creek on Church Neck. Birdsnest flies north a mile or so and becomes an ordinary on the Seaside Road. Exmore is axed altogether. Keller and Painter move into the retirement home for forgotten railroad

CURTIS J. BADGER

Necks of Accomack County

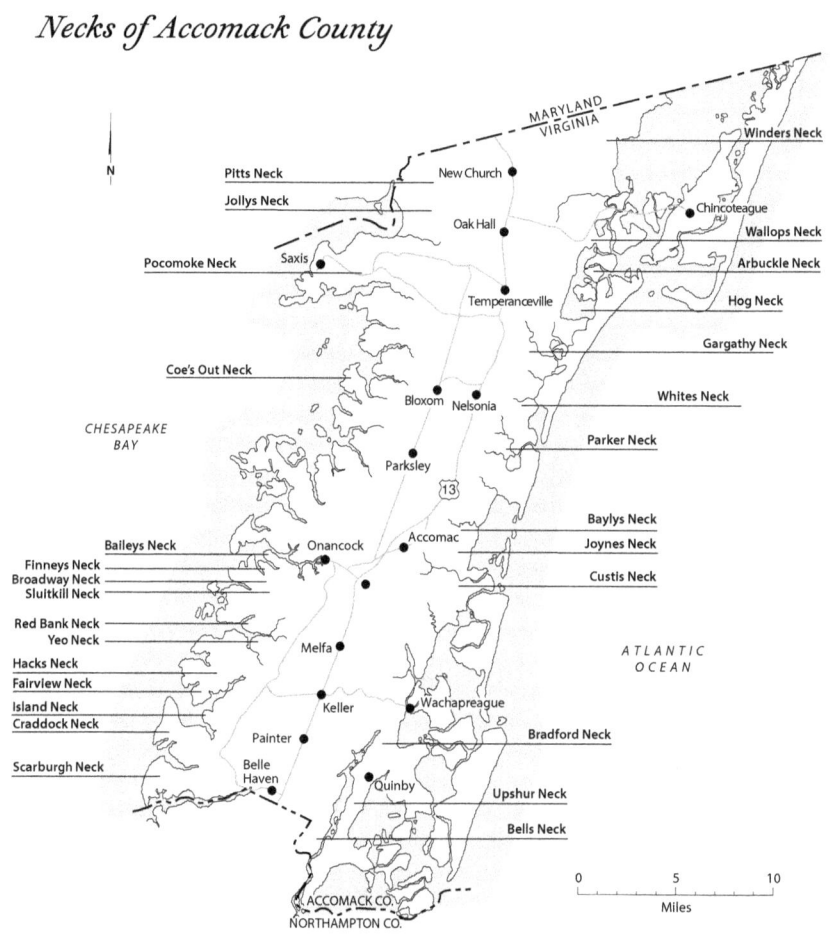

Bill Nelson Cartography

executives. Melfa becomes a river in Italy and the scene of a major World War II battle. Onley forfeits an "e" and is again the home of the first Virginia governor from Onancock Creek.

On we go. Parksley was the invention of the railroad, a planned community. No more planned communities. Parksley is now fertile fields where Mr. Benjamin Parks grows corn and oats. Bloxom and Tasley carry Keller and Painter's baggage to the retirement home, and earn a nice tip. We'll roll it all back to the Pocomoke River, the mighty Pocomoke, blackwater beauty, where our quest ends.

Introduction

Like archaeologists, we have skimmed away the primary layer and have exposed what lies beneath. Now, what are we left with, other than about 20,000 people with no place to live and no way to get there? We have the Eastern Shore as it was in the fall of 1883. The population was about 15,000 in Accomack and 7,000 in Northampton, so we can scuttle the twenty thousand railroaders. They were in too much of a hurry anyway.

Everyone moves back to the water, to the wooded, fertile high lands that separate the creeks and line the bays. People grow things. They build ships and travel to other places along the bay and along the Atlantic coast. They cut timber and send it to cities to help build houses for the twenty thousand we scuttled. They grow corn and oats and take them to mills at the heads of creeks, where they are ground and taken home to make bread.

The high lands that separate bodies of water are called necks, necks of the woods, and they were America's first residential communities. They were the product of evolution, not planning. People came, looking for a home, and they found one in their neck of the woods. Some of the people who settled in the necks were related, others friends, all dependent upon one another. Some of the English families that settled in the necks in the 17th century still have relatives there, and the names are familiar within the landscape.

In 1883 the Eastern Shore had at least three dozen named necks, communities where people lived. In order to survive, a neck needed two things: a wharf to facilitate travel and trade, and an established community to offer common services for residents and visitors. These typically included a church, an ordinary or inn, merchants, a blacksmith, tanner, and perhaps an apothecary. These communities were usually located at the head of the neck, away from the water, and they were linked to other necks by roads and footpaths.

Most of these "heads of the neck" still exist, although many of the structures have long since weathered away. On the bayside, for example, the heads of the neck would include Pungoteague, Craddockville (formerly Turkey Pens), Belle Haven, Hadlock, Franktown, Bridgetown,

Necks of Northampton County

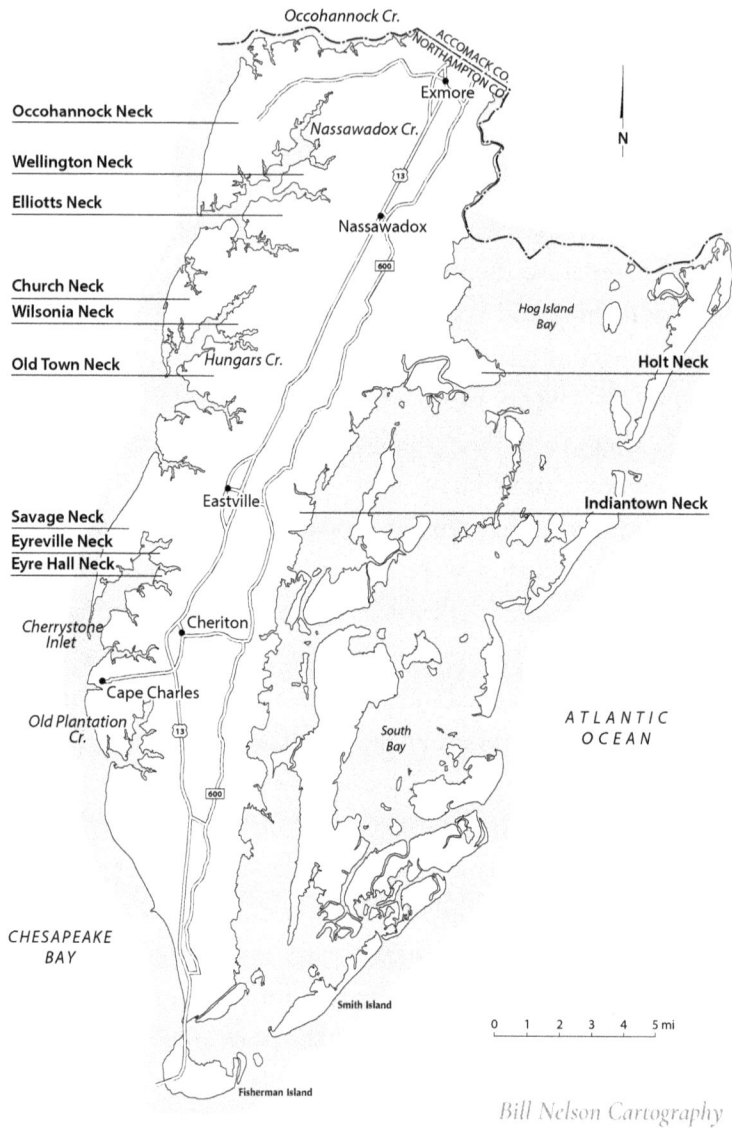

Johnsontown, and Machipongo, or Shadyside, the head of Wilsonia Neck. The roads that connect these villages today run along the same route that linked them in 1883 and long before that. Prior to 1883, these were the population centers of the Eastern Shore.

INTRODUCTION

A similar network of necks linked by stagecoach routes and pathways exists on the seaside. Quinby (Warwick Plantation prior to the railroad) is the head of Upshur Neck, Wachapreague (formerly Powellton, and before that Teackles Landing) is the head of Bradford Neck, Daugherty (formerly Bull Run) the head of Custis Neck, Assawoman the head of Arbuckle Neck, Wattsville the head of Wallops Neck, and Horntown the head of Winders Neck.

The bayside and seaside stagecoach routes are connected here and there to facilitate travel across the peninsula. Onley, as it became known in railroad days, was along one such bay-to-sea junction. Prior to 1884 the community was known fittingly as Crossroads. It linked Onancock on the west with Locustville on the east.

The town of Nassawadox, which was an important railroad station for upper Northampton County, got its name from a location at the head of Hungars Creek now known as Bridgetown, in Church Neck. The Native Americans called the area Nussawattox to describe an area of land (Church Neck) between two waters. When Nassawadox became a railroad station in the center of the peninsula, everyone assumed the definition described the town's location between the Chesapeake Bay and the Atlantic Ocean. That is not what the Native Americans had in mind. The term Nussawattox was used by the natives to describe a neck of land.

*This is Taylor Creek near the community of Pungoteague. On the left (south) side of the creek is Hacks Neck and Harborton, and on the right side is Yeo Neck and the Eastern Shore Yacht and Country Club.
Aerial photograph courtesy of Gordon Campbell, At Altitude Gallery.*

Peninsulas in Repose

My daughter-in-law in Oregon collects words. Specifically, she collects words that are old and seldom used anymore but still manage to evoke an image that is unique and thought provoking. When she finds such a word, she shares it with family and friends. Her word-gift recently was "demi-isle," a word that was used to describe a peninsula before peninsula became part of the English language.

Her favorite source of antiquated words is a book written in 2000 by Jeffrey Kacirk titled *The Word Museum – The Most Remarkable English Words Ever Forgotten*. Demi-isle appears on page 53, sandwiched between deepmusing, which means "in thoughtful meditation," and dendanthropology, which is a study based on the premise that man evolved from trees.

She knows that we live on a peninsula, or demi-isle, and I told her that our large peninsula is actually made up of many small peninsulas, which we call "necks." Delmarva is obviously and emphatically a peninsula, with the Atlantic on one side and the Chesapeake on the other, but within the bounds of Delmarva are dozens of tracts of land that meet the definition of peninsula. That is, a narrow strip of land surrounded on two or three sides by water. And, unlike the Delmarva peninsula, most necks are not arranged vertically, north and south, but horizontally, like peninsulas in repose.

Eastern Shore necks are a complement to our seaside islands and bayside beaches and marsh meadows. The English settled in wooded areas along the coast that were accessed by navigable creeks and streams, and as the population grew, wooded necks became the places where people chose to live. Necks became the original American community. The "neck of the woods" was your home.

"Any bears where you live?"

"Never seen one in our neck of the woods."

In the early years, people settled in the wooded necks where land was fertile and dry. Sheep, cattle, and horses were pastured on the barrier islands and bayside marshes, and animals adjusted to a natural diet of spartina grasses, shrubs, and vines such as greenbrier. As long as fresh water was available, the animals did fine. Pasturing animals on islands saved greatly on feed costs, and it kept them out of fields where planters were attempting to grow corn, tobacco, and other crops.

Towns are a comparatively modern concept on the Eastern Shore, many a product of the railroad, which began rolling in 1884. Necks do not show up on state highway maps or county road maps, although road signs still let you know you're travelling on Upshur Neck Road, or perhaps Arbuckle Neck Road. Google Earth does identify many

necks, but the best way to vicariously explore our necks is to get out the venerable and reliable U.S. Geological Survey topo maps. Most are based on aerial photographs taken more than 50 years ago, but necks are reasonably stable landforms that rarely move great distances.

No one seems to know the origin of the term "neck," but it has been around for a long time. The easy assumption is that it was imported by the English when they colonized the region in the early 1600s, but my friends Terry and Judy Malarkey, who are from England, say they had never heard of the term until moving to the Eastern Shore. One theory is that the English purposely assigned new names to landforms in the new world. Rather than using traditional English terms such as heath, moor, fen, and dell, they came up with hollow, gap, branch, neck, and gut – new, uniquely American names.

Exactly when the English settlers began referring to their home as a neck is the great unknown. Perhaps they used the old term demi-isle, but the historians I have spoken with do not recall seeing that term in the written records. Perhaps in the early days they simply used a nautical reference. "We're building on land we patented on Old Plantation Creek." It probably took the settlers some time to get a feel for the lay of the land, something that came gradually through exploring their home on foot and by water. In the early years, the emphasis was on survival, not geography.

The Eastern Shore has some forty named necks on the seaside and bayside, beginning on the south with Old Plantation Neck, which is bordered by Old Plantation and Kings Creek. Farther north are Eyre Hall and Eyreville Necks, and Savage Neck in Northampton County. The northernmost neck is Winders Neck in upper Accomack, which is defined by the waters of Swans Gut Creek, Coldkill Creek, and Chincoteague Bay.

As noted earlier, most of our necks are peninsulas in repose, created by creeks that run perpendicular to the spine of the Eastern Shore. Notable exceptions are Bradford Neck, Upshur Neck, and Bells Neck, which are parallel to each other, and separated by Hog Island Bay, Machipongo River, and Parting Creek, from east to west.

The Franktown area on the bayside is threaded by numerous waterways and thus has many necks, including, from north to south, Occohannock, Wellington, Elliotts, Church, Wilsonia, Old Town, and Great Neck. The necks are formed by the Nassawadox, Church, Hungars, Jacobus, Savage, and Mattawoman Creeks and their tributaries.

The Shore's link with space exploration, NASA's Wallops Flight Facility, is located on Wallops Neck, a product of waterways that include Mosquito Creek, Little Mosquito Creek, Simoneaston Bay, and Simoneaston Creek.

Most of the necks on the Shore reflect the names of the original patent holders of land, or those of families who had substantial acreage. These include families who were prominent in Eastern Shore history, with names such as Savage, Custis, Upshur, Scarburgh, Wallop, White, Joynes, Bayly, Bell, Brickhouse, Parker, Arbuckle, and Hack. Many of the necks are created by waterways with names reflecting the Native American presence, but most of the necks are named for English settlers.

The necks more closely resemble ribs than they do necks. If the backbone of the Eastern Shore is its spine, running more or less north and south, then the necks are ribs. stretching from the open water of the Chesapeake Bay and the Broadwater of the seaside inland toward the spine. In the years before the railroad drew people to the spine of the Shore, the area was densely wooded. We had necks of the woods on the seaside and bayside, separated by navigable waterways. The forested area that ran along the spine of the Eastern Shore was referred to as the mid-woods, according to historian Brooks Miles Barnes.

Necks were the original communities of the Eastern Shore, easily accessible by water to facilitate trade and travel, populated by people with a common bond; they lived and worked in the same neck of land. Early colonists chose as homesites wooded land that was near navigable water. The Native Americans preferred land that had fertile soil, fresh water for drinking and cooking, and they valued fresh water or brackish wetlands rather than deep water for navigation. In those wetlands grew grasses and reeds the people used for making tools and baskets, and in the swamps they found emergent plants such as arum, whose roots were used in cooking.

Necks are communities defined by natural boundaries, not political ones. It is often difficult to say exactly where a neck begins, but it is certain as to where it ends. When your feet get wet, you have reached the boundary. Necks have no geo-political infrastructure. There is no mayor and council and most are not named on maps. What they do have is a colorful history; some were home to early political leaders and influential people within the colony. Others had a dark side. Sluitkill Neck, near Cashville, was the scene of a grisly murder in 1885.

Living on a neck in the early days of settlement was not unlike living on an island. Isolation brought people closer through social and familial bonds. Typically, a neck would be populated by families that had large landholdings, but gradually, as more people moved onto the land and as families expanded, the population became more diverse. Early settlers did not follow the tradition of primogeniture, in which land is left to the eldest son, so large families meant that family land would be divided numerous times over the generations. In addition, life expectancy was comparatively short, so land was often transferred during re-marriages.

Although the necks were isolated from the mainland, there was a great sense of community within the neck itself. James R. Perry, in his book *The Formation of a Society on Virginia's Eastern Shore, 1615-1655*, writes that social cohesion was very strong, with people providing for both family members and neighbors. "People turned to their neighbors for an exchange of sociability and favors as well as responsibilities," he wrote. "Individually and collectively, neighbors also exercised a degree of social control. This skein of interactions helped to bind landowners together on the Eastern Shore."

The necks along the seaside and bayside offered everything settlers needed, so there was little interest in moving to the central spine, the mid-woods. The water provided food and a means of travel, and a social network provided contact with family and friends as well as security.

"A century and a half ago (circa 1800) the Virginia Eastern Shore's communities were almost entirely on or not far from the bayside creeks or the seaside inlets," wrote James Egbert Mears in the 1950 anthology *The Eastern Shore – Maryland and Virginia*. "There were few villages in the center of the peninsula until after 1884, with the completion of the New York, Philadelphia and Norfolk Railroad; in fact, when it began operating it passed through not a single village between New Church and the new town of Cape Charles."

Necks are a geological phenomenon, the serendipitous placement of high land near deep water. The great majority of Eastern Shore necks are on the bayside of Northampton County and the seaside of Accomack. Northampton's seaside is noted for its vast Broadwater, miles of shallow water, marshy islands, tidal flats, and meandering channels. When a blue-eyed British dandy explored the area looking for a place to settle, the high banks of Nassawadox Creek had vastly more appeal than a seaside mud flat.

The converse is true in Accomack. The northern county's bayside is a maze of tidal creeks threading vast spartina marshes, interrupted

Bayside Marsh

Bayside Hammock

Saxis Marsh

now and then by marginal high lands called hammocks, or hummocks, most of them an acre or two of stunted pine, cedar, holly, wax myrtle, and groundsel. It is a beautiful landscape, but not given to growing corn and tobacco.

Accomack's necks are clustered along the seaside, where the barrier islands hug the mainland and tidal creeks meander into fertile, sandy soil. Folly Creek was the avenue by which most seaside residents reached the county seat, then known as Drummondtown. Ten named necks lie on the seaside from Accomac north, and most of them recognize prominent landowners and leaders. The names could be taken from the index of a book on Eastern Shore history. There is Custis, Joynes, Baylys, Parkers, Whites, Arbuckle, Wallops, and Winders. They are joined by Gargathy, which is derived from Gargaphia, the name of a colonial era plantation, and Hog, which reflects the ancient practice of pasturing animals on the islands, marshes, and necks. In Accomack, we have Hog Island, Hog Neck, Hog Creek, and Hog Neck Creek. Hog Neck is huge, Accomack's largest neck, a great sprawling landscape of forest and saltmarsh stretching from Gargathy Creek north to Assawoman Creek.

Although Accomack has Pitts Neck and Jollys Neck near the northern boundary, most of the necks on the bayside begin south of the marshlands of Saxis, Cattail Neck, and Parkers Marsh. An exception would be Coe's Out Neck, an area between Muddy Creek and Guilford Creek settled by Timothy Coe around 1660. The tract is mostly marshland, but Coe built a plantation on the high land and supposedly had a lumber mill on the property. The head of Coe's Out Neck would have been the community of Guilford, one of the oldest settlements in Accomack County. Another exception would be Pocomoke Neck, which lies between Holden and Messongo Creeks. It was also referred to as Freeschool Neck and Messongo Neck.

The majority of the bayside necks begin on the south shore of Onancock Creek with Baileys Neck, Finneys Neck (There also is Finneys Creek and Finneys Island.), Broadway Neck, and Sluitkill Neck, which is accessed by Tarkill Road. Sluitkill implies perhaps a Dutch influence ("kill" meaning small creek in Dutch.), But spellings in various old publications and records vary greatly, including Sluthkill, Slutkiln, Slutkill, and various others.

South of Onancock Creek, the bayside necks are relatively well-defined. Yeo Neck, home of the Eastern Shore Yacht and Country Club, is formed by Pungoteague and Taylor Creeks. Between Pungoteague Creek and Nandua Creek lies Hacks Neck, which is probably the only Eastern Shore neck to have a book published about it. *Hacks Neck and Its People, Past and Present*, a history and genealogy of the George Hack family and their associates, was published in 1937 by James Egbert Mears. Pungoteague was the head of Hacks Neck, with the requisite churches, inns, bars, stores, and other improvements.

If you take Rt. 178 from Pungoteague south to Craddockville, you will skirt the eastern boundaries of Fairview Neck, Island Neck, Craddock Neck and Scarburgh Neck. Craddock Neck lies between Nandua Creek and Craddock Creek and consists mainly of farmland and woodland. If you keep straight on Rt. 615 instead bearing left on Rt. 178, you will soon be in Scarburgh Neck. The road comes to an abrupt end at a boatyard in Davis Wharf, one of the ancient landings on Occohannock Creek. Look across the creek and you will see Morley's Wharf (formerly Read's Wharf), an equally ancient landing serving the residents of Occohannock Neck in Northampton County. Davis Wharf and Morley's Wharf served the farming communities of Scarburgh Neck and Occohannock Neck from the early days of settlement until the railroad and motor truck gradually supplanted sail and steamboats as the preferred method of getting farm produce to markets and city goods to rural homes.

Scarburgh Neck is larger than Craddock Neck, and Occohannock is larger than both. Occohannock Creek flows deeply into the Eastern Shore peninsula, separating the two counties. Its upper branches (Taylor Branch is the largest.) reach almost to Rt. 13 and north to the pond at the Agricultural Experiment Station near Painter. Occohannock Neck is a mixture of agriculture and residential use, and it is known by generations of Eastern Shore residents for its beaches.

Silver Beach has been a popular summer community for years and a gathering spot for young people from both counties.

Unlike most of the necks farther north, Occohannock has a great deal of high, fertile land, making it one of the leading farming communities on the Eastern Shore. The neck is bordered on the north by Occohannock Creek, on the west by Chesapeake Bay, and on the south by Nassawadox Creek. The prominent shoreline, fertile soil, and the nearness of deep water made it a favorite of early settlers. Drive through the farm fields and glance at the meandering waters of Nassawadox Creek far below, and the appeal of the landscape is obvious.

When the railroad opened on the Eastern Shore in 1884 the great productivity of Occohannock Neck farms made a compelling case for extending a 12-mile spur line from Exmore through the communities of Wardtown and Jamesville to mine the wealth of truck crops grown in the region. But the rail spur never materialized, and farmers continued to send crops to market by sail and steam, running from landings situated where navigable waters neared high land. Some of the busiest wharves were Morley's, Concord, Shield's, and Rue's on Occohannock Creek.

The opening of the railroad, and the possibility of a spur line down Occohannock Neck, created competition between the railroad and local shippers. William J. Rue, who operated a wharf near Belle Haven, published a shipping schedule in the *Peninsula Enterprise*, the local weekly newspaper. In September 1885 Mr. Rue ran the following announcement:

> The safe delivery of every barrel of produce is guaranteed by me, the dangers of the sea excepted. Sort your potatoes well, fill your barrels full, and don't let the hot sun burn them at the time of digging them, ship them by my vessels according to my instructions, and I will guarantee satisfaction or as good returns as shipped by any other route. I will always be ready to buy at the wharf for cash or goods, and will pay the highest prices for good stock. Patronize your home friends.

One of the advantages of living and farming on a neck was that navigable water was near and accessible and there were always vessels to be had. Many farmers in Northampton County shipped their own potatoes simply by loading them onto private vessels and taking them to the railroad pier in Cape Charles City to sell directly to buyers.

When the market for white potatoes was at its strongest in the first decade of the 20th century, Cape Charles was a busy, thriving port, with a constant flow of vessels of all shapes and sizes bringing barrels of potatoes from the farm to the railroad. The peak of the white potato season was late June and early July, and the railroad during this time was shipping potatoes as fast as they could load them, which to some of the growers was not fast enough.

On June 29, 1907 a writer with the *Norfolk Landmark* filed this report:

> On Thursday the New York, Philadelphia and Norfolk railroad sent out from that point (Cape Charles City) no less than 12,000 barrels, according to the shipping clerk's figures, and yesterday there were sent out almost as many. Still the cry is for more cars and some complain of the railroad, whether justly or not, for not handling them faster.
>
> There were one hundred sail vessels from Old Plantation, Hungars and Occohannock creeks anchored in the harbor awaiting their turn to unload yesterday afternoon. The greater number of these had to wait over until today. In the meantime, a large number of others constantly arrived until night fall.
>
> The farmers usually go down with the vessels and try to make sales on the dock. This in part accounts for the delay in handling the product. For this a potato exchange wharf would be a great convenience and it would enable the farmer to get his crop handled and at the same time relieve the congestion on the rail road wharf. Next week will see the biggest rush from this section.

The history of European settlement on Virginia's Eastern Shore is generally divided into periods ranging from early contact years, through formation of a society, the period of trade by sail, by steam, by railroad, and by highway. Our history has been marked by how we trade and how we travel, how we do business. These factors have determined where we live, what we grow and gather, and how we make profit from it. The necks of the Eastern Shore have been a part of all of these periods. Our necks, our peninsulas in repose, demonstrate that geology and geography play a great role in determining where we live and how we conduct trade and how we travel. The earliest setters were drawn to the necks because deep water made them accessible, and the fertile, sandy soil offered promise of wealth. And now, in our fifth century of settlement, we still find great value in our neck of the woods.

Old Plantation and a White Man Called Savage

The first settlements on the Eastern Shore were on the southern tip of the peninsula, in the Magothy area on the seaside and in Old Plantation, Eyre Hall, and Eyreville Necks along the lower bayside in Northampton. Early settlers found that the deep creeks of the bayside and the relatively high land aided in travel and commerce, using Cherrystone Inlet as the avenue of ingress and egress.

This area on the tip of the peninsula is being closely studied today by historians and archaeologists because the land has seen little change over the four centuries since the first English colonists arrived. There still are large farms and significant tracts of public land protected as state park, natural area preserves, and national wildlife refuges. In addition, important private holdings are protected via conservation easements. Scientists know that the southern tip of the Eastern Shore is a vital resting stop on the avian flyway, providing birds a place to rest and refuel as they migrate along the east coast corridor. The advantages of protecting these places have been recognized by historians as well, as we learn important details about rural life in the colonial period.

One such example deserves special mention, and that is Eyre Hall, the ancestral home of the Baldwin and Eyre families, wealthy landowners and business leaders whose plantation, built in 1759, is a very rare example of a home still being occupied by the descendants of the original builder. The plantation lies on a neck of land bordered by Eyre Hall Creek on the south and Eyreville Creek on the north. The western portion of the neck faces Cherrystone Creek.

The plantation was built by Littleton Eyre and is currently

occupied by the Furlong Baldwin family, who graciously share the gardens with the public. The home is a regular on the Garden Tour held each spring, and it provides an unprecedented look at a home occupied by the same family for many generations. The furniture, artwork, artifacts, and other household items are all original to the family and have been collected by them over the generations since 1759.

The Eyres and Baldwins were local planters, but they were active in business in Baltimore, and over the years Eyre Hall became their country home, a comfortable and familiar home away from the city. The city home is where they entertained, built business relationships, and maintained a glossy public image of wealth and privilege. As a result, Eyre Hall prospered from a sort of benign neglect, evolving into a rare jewel, a living example of colonial history, not one that has been recreated.

The Maryland Center for History and Culture published an exceptional book on Eyre Hall in 2021 titled *The Material World of Eyre Hall – Four Centuries of Chesapeake History*. It is highly recommended.

When the English first settled on the Eastern Shore, one of their primary missions was to support the original colony across the bay at James City. This was accomplished by distilling salt from sea water to preserve food, and by catching fish and growing crops to help feed the colony.

Dale's Gift was established by James City officials as a land base to service the salt work on Smith Island, and it is not known exactly where it was located, but most historians seem to focus on the lands around Old Plantation, where the first settlers established a community.

An option would be a site on the seaside at the very tip of the peninsula where the Eastern Shore of Virginia National Wildlife Refuge and the Chesapeake Bay Bridge-Tunnel headquarters are located today. If, indeed, the purpose of Dale's Gift was to service the salt-making facility on Smith Island, it would have made more sense to locate it on the eastern side of the peninsula rather than the western. One can stand at the boat landing at the refuge and easily see Smith Island in the distance. It would have been a much shorter, quicker run from the mainland to the island than having to sail around the tip and north up the bay to Old Plantation.

At the time the colonists arrived from James City, Fisherman Island had not yet formed at the southern tip of the Eastern Shore. Instead, it was a vast area of shoal water, only a few feet deep, and navigating it with the wind from the north would have been treacherous. Vessels would have had to make a wide sweep of the cape to avoid the shoals, thus making the trip quite a bit longer from Smith Island to Old Plantation, had that been the site of Dale's Gift. It makes sense that they would have used a more direct route.

While Dale's Gift and other similar encampments were temporary by nature, the land of the first permanent settlement is thought to have been on Savage Neck, named for Thomas Savage, a young man who lived among the native people and provided invaluable service to the James City government by acting as a translator and diplomat in dealing with the natives.

Savage Neck is arguably the most spectacular of the forty or so named necks on the Eastern Shore. It has everything a proper neck should have, and yet more. Savage Neck has human history. Road signs tout it as the home of the Eastern Shore's first English settler. Savage Neck has natural history. A dune ridge stretching for a mile along the bay is protected by the state as the Savage Neck Dunes Natural Area Preserve (NAP). Savage Neck has historic homes and churches, it has incredible waterfront vistas, and it has the county seat whose offices hold the oldest continuous court records in America.

Local folks of a certain age usually refer to Savage Neck as Sand Hills, so named for the unusual landscape of vast secondary dunes lying just east of the primary dunes fronting the Chesapeake. Sand Hills has been the site of family picnics for generations, and rumor has it that young people would sometimes gather there in the evenings for a bit of socializing. Just north of Sand Hills is Wilkins Beach, home of a well-known hotel of another era where local people gathered for dances and parties. The hotel closed around the time of World War II, and all that remains are a few photographs and memories, both of which are fading.

Savage Neck is a fascinating landscape that sparks the imagination.

Wilkins Beach Hotel

Wilkins Beach Hotel

Old Plantation and a White Man Called Savage

Thomas Savage, at age 13, is said to have come to live with the Native Americans on Savage Neck and remained with them for three years, consumed by their language and culture. As an adult, he was a valuable emissary who bridged the gap between the English newcomers and the natives. His sense of diplomacy likely saved lives among all parties.

Geologists and botanists could make a career of studying Savage Neck. The dune ridge is unlike anything else on the Eastern Shore, with high peaks dropping steeply into forests below. How did this land form evolve? Was it part of an ancient barrier island dune system? And what of the pond, Custis Pond, a naturally occurring freshwater lagoon surrounded by dunes and forest? It could have, at one time, millennia ago, been an ocean inlet that divided barrier islands and allowed the passage of ocean water into the saltmarshes of the broadwater. Yes, Savage Neck does make one wonder.

The neck begins on the north where an estuary called The Gulf separates it from Old Town Neck. The Gulf, once known as Savage Creek, runs inland for several miles from its confluence with the bay, years ago reaching all the way to the county seat at Eastville, which afforded residents convenient transportation for conducting court business. It has since silted in considerably and its upper reaches are not navigable.

The neck has about seventeen miles of shoreline along the bay, running from The Gulf south to Wescoat's Point, a sandy spit on Cherrystone Inlet across from the campground. Cherrystone Inlet and Old Castle Creek form the southern and eastern boundaries, with Eyreville Neck neighboring on the south. Eastville, the seat of governance, is the head of the neck.

The accessibility of Savage Neck to deep water made the area very desirable during the colonial period, and many historic homes are tucked away at the heads of creeks, on farms, and in Eastville itself. The homes of Savage Neck make up a large section of Ralph T. Whitelaw's *Virginia's Eastern Shore*. Section N49 will take you through everything from Thomas Savage's relationship with Debdeavon and Pocahontas to the opening of the Eastville Inn.

The life and times of Thomas Savage provide one of the more compelling stories of the early English settlement on the Eastern Shore. Generations of school children were taught in Virginia history that Thomas Savage was the first permanent English resident of the Eastern Shore, who lived among the Native Americans as an adolescent and learned their language. A road sign erected by the Virginia Department of Historic Resources ("Home of the First Settler") on U.S. Rt. 13 (Bus.) near Savage Neck Road tells us that Thomas arrived in Jamestown on January 2, 1608 in the ship *John and Francis*, whose captain was Christopher Newport. Thomas was 13 at the time. The sign quotes John Smith as saying "A boy name Thomas Savage (whom Newport called son) was then given unto Powhatan." Savage resided with the Indians for several years, "growing up in association with Pocahontas."

According to the sign, Thomas became fluent in the native languages and often served as an interpreter in dealings involving the colonists and native people. Thomas was given "perhaps 9,000" acres of land by Debdeavon, the "Laughing King," for increasing trade with the Indians."

New studies have cast some doubt on the "first settler" claim, and many historians today say that Thomas Savage provided great services to the colony at James City regarding negotiations with the native people, and he was indeed an early settler on the Shore, although probably not the first, and the land he was given was probably less than 9,000 acres. The story of Thomas Savage is engrossing but it is probably derived from folklore, which repeated often enough, becomes accepted as fact. Historians are still looking for evidence from a reliable primary source that Savage came to live with the Native Americans as a boy and became the first permanent resident.

Jenean Hall, in her 2022 book, *An "Uncertaine Rumor" of Land – New Thoughts on the English Founding of Virginia's Eastern Shore*, makes a good case that John and Frances Blore were the first settlers.

Whitelaw wrote that historians are not even sure whether Savage was the correct name. Some accounts say Thomas was the son of

Christopher Newport; others claim that his name was derived from his close association with "savages," having lived among them for several years.

The Thomas Savage story seems to be another example of what may be a peculiarly American compulsion to name someone or something number one. In every endeavor, it seems, it is necessary to have a first. First to fly, first to walk on the moon, first to climb Everest, first to reach the South Pole, first to discover America.

Many of us were taught in school that Christopher Columbus was the first to discover America. He was a heroic figure and a federal holiday was established in his honor. We later realized that Columbus was neither the first nor was he necessarily heroic. The colonization of North America was a process that evolved in fits and starts; it did not happen one day in 1492, and it was not the achievement of one man.

We have been conditioned to record history through linking firsts and dates. We are taught the name and date of the man who discovered America, or the battles of the Civil War, or those of World War II, but we overlook the complexities of the issues. It makes testing easy. It is not difficult to memorize and regurgitate dates and places; it is more challenging to analyze trends that evolve over years and centuries.

Nevertheless, Thomas Savage served the colony and the Eastern Shore well, and he can with certainty be named the first of many Savages to call The Eastern Shore home. It is a family that has served the community with distinction for four centuries.

English Customs Become American Ways

Life on the Eastern Shore centered on the water. It was part of everyday life. Tidal creeks, bays, and the ocean connected the Eastern Shore with the rest of the world. In addition, the creeks and bays were a great source of food, which fed the family and provided income. Most necks had at least one wharf, or landing, which acted as the focal point for imports and exports. A few of these remain, but most are long gone, some sites marked only by a few pilings haphazardly scattered along a fringe of saltmarsh. The road signs are still there, the only tangible evidence of an earlier era. Evans Wharf Road, Boggs Wharf Road, Finneys Wharf Road, Morley's Wharf Road. Only the latter is still in the wharf business. Northampton County maintains a boat launch there, along with a popular fishing pier. Across Occohannock Creek from Morley's Wharf lies Davis Wharf, at the end of Davis Wharf Road, another port site that dates back centuries.

Eastern Shore necks, wooded areas of high land adjacent to navigable water, were the first lands to be settled by the English immigrants. Necks were on both the seaside and bayside, and the spine of the Eastern Shore, the area where commerce is centered today, was unfamiliar territory during the era of necks. When people visited the Eastern Shore, whether for commerce or social interaction, they came by water, did their business, and returned by water. There was little reason to explore the mid-woods beyond the community at the head of the neck.

Most of the early settlers came from the English countryside, and they brought with them many of the customs and manners of their

native land. John S. Wise, son of Gov. Henry A. Wise, wrote in his memoir, *The End of an Era*, (Houghton, Mifflin Co. 1900) "Nowhere is the type of the original settler in Virginia so well preserved, or are to be found the antique customs, manners, and ways of the Englishman of the seventeenth century in America so little altered, as in the Kingdom of Accawmacke. No considerable influx of population from anywhere else has ever gone to the eastern shore of Virginia since the year 1700. The names of the very earliest settlers are still there."

Wise explained that the necks were created by creeks that separated the land by only a short distance in many places, but villages were separated by land often by great distances. "These numerous inlets, many of which are navigable for vessels of considerable size, are but a few miles apart, and divide the Peninsula into many transverse "necks," he wrote. "Thus, it often happens that neighbors living on opposite sides of these creeks, within hailing distance of each other, find it necessary, in order to visit each other by land, to travel miles around the head of the creek dividing them."

Wise noted that English names were used to identify necks and creeks on the southern part of the Eastern Shore, while native terms were used farther north. "On the bayside, going northward from the cape where the oldest settlements were made, the names of these creeks are English, such as Old Plantation, Cherrystone, and Hungars. Higher up the bayside, the names given by the Indians before the white settlements seem to have been retained; for we have successively Occohannock, Nandua, Pungoteague, Onancock, Chesconnessex, Annamessex, and Pocomoke as the names of the beautiful and bold insets on the bay side. On the seaside, they rejoice in such titles as Assawoman, Chincoteague, and the like."

The customs of the English survived a war of independence and various skirmishes since then, and are evident even to the present day. My family came from England and were planters in Virginia, and I would bet they tilled the land back in whatever shire they left. My grandmother married a farmer and was the daughter of a farmer, and she brought English customs to her family farm on Red Bank Creek. She frequently referred to an area on the farm as the "pound yard," a word I had never heard before or since. She was speaking of the part of the farm separate from the formal yard and garden, but not part of the tilled land. In the pound yard were the barn and workshop, the equipment shed, corn crib, hen house, and various other structures critical to farming the land. The hog lot was in the pound yard as well, but situated a considerable distance from the house.

The necks are where ancient English customs gradually blended with new Eastern Shore ways and therefore became a distinctive part of our coastal culture. The ability to handle a boat was a given, and boat building became a distinct expression that blended the practical needs of travel with the pleasure of pleasing the eye. Boats were like duck decoys, intended to both please the eye and perform a function. Wrote Wise: "Small boats are, therefore, as much in use as means of intercourse between neighbors, and for visiting the post offices and little towns at the wharves, as are horses and vehicles; and an eastern shore man is as much at home in a boat as upon the land."

A graphic example of the arrangement of necks, waterways, and

English Customs Become American Ways

villages can be found in old maps, most of which came from atlases of North America. The David Rumsey online collection (www.davidrumsey.com) includes numerous maps depicting Virginia and Maryland, and if you zoom in on particular maps, much detail can be seen. A map of Virginia, Maryland, and North Carolina was made by Johann Baptist Homann in 1720 and published in an atlas in Nuremberg, Germany. The necks are clearly delineated, especially on Northampton County's bayside, and are identified only by number, which probably references an accompanying text. The Eastern Shore of Virginia includes three counties –Northampton, Accomack, and Arcadia – and Virginia's Eastern Shore is shown as part of Maryland. No town names are given, but Teches Island (probably Parramore), Matthapunko Island (probably Hog), and Chincoteague Island are shown.

Also from the Rumsey collection is a map made by Henry S. Tanner in 1833 of Virginia, Maryland, and Delaware. Principal towns include Horntown, Drummondtown, Onancock, Pungoteague, Franktown,

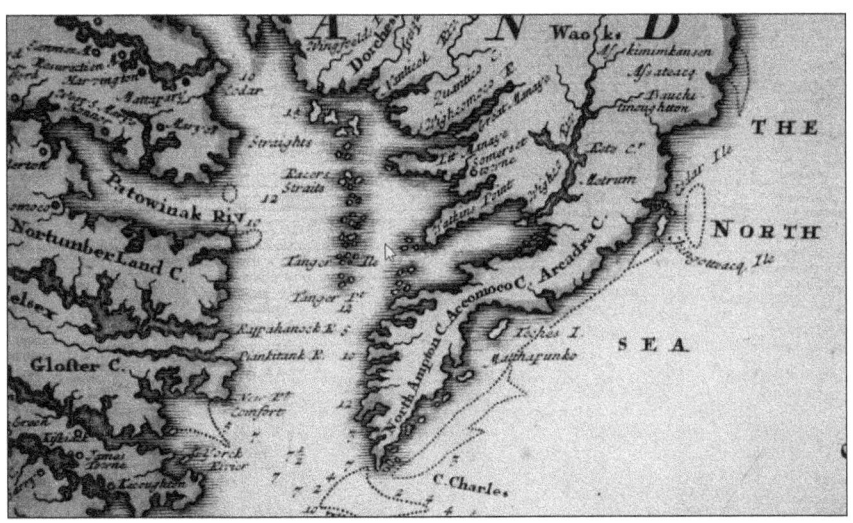

1720 Homann Map

This 1720 map by Homann shows the Eastern Shore as being part of Maryland and having three counties: Northampton, Accomack, and Arcadia. Courtesy of the David Rumsey Collection of Stanford University.

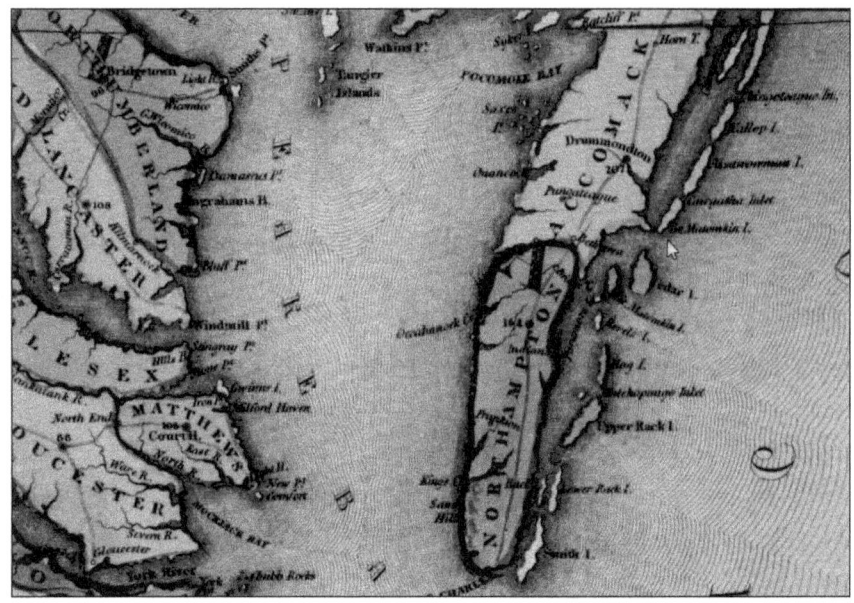

An 1833 map by Henry S. Tanner shows little detail of the central part of the Eastern Shore, which was virtually unexplored during that period. Tanner does include great detail of the coast. Courtesy of the David Rumsey Collection of Stanford University.

Kings Creek, Sand Hills, Bridgetown, and Belle Haven (which was nspelled Beth Haven). Eastville, the county seat, was identified only by the number 164, which probably references to a guide in the atlas. No detail is shown of the central spine of the Eastern Shore, but a roadway is shown running north and south, which probably reflects guesswork on Tanner's part. It is obvious that cartographers were unfamiliar with the portion of the Eastern Shore away from the water, even as late as 1833. Local historian Brooks Miles Barnes says that during this period the central part of the Shore was, to most, *terra incognita*, unknown territory, a part of Virginia that remained generally unexplored long after the Revolution.

Tanner did know the seaside, though. He identified Assateague Island, Chincoteague, Wallops, Assawoman, Gargatha Inlet, Metompkin, Cedar, Little Machipongo Inlet, Hog, Revels, Upper Rack (Wreck) Island, Lower Rack, and Smith Island. No mention is made of Myrtle or Ship Shoal because they had not yet broken off from Smith Island.

A more modern map takes us to the dawn of the railroad era. It was made by Samuel A. Mitchell in 1884 and published in an atlas by William Bradley & Bro. of Philadelphia. The map features prominently the route of the NYP&N Railroad and the connecting routes of the Eastern Shore Railroad and Worcester Railroad in Maryand. More than thirty towns and villages were identified, but only Chincoteague and Cobbs Islands were recognized. The map was likely commissioned by Pennsylvania Railroad.

Eastern Shore towns prominently shown on maps in the pre-railroad era include some of our oldest communities, many of which were heads of necks or wharfs associated with necks. In Accomack, these include Pitts Wharf, Horntown, Sandfordville (Sanford), Atlantic, Guilford (one of the oldest), Modest Town, Metompkin, Drummondtown, Locustville, Locust Mount, Hoffman's Wharf (Harborton), Belle Haven, and Davis Wharf.

In Northampton, from north to south, prominent communities include Hadlock, Concord Wharf, Wardtown, Franktown, Marionville, Bridgetown, Shadyside, Wilsonia Wharf, Eastville, Cherrystone, Sea View, and Capeville. Cape Charles City came along in 1884.

Towns and villages were named on many maps, but the location was often suspect. Franktown and Bridgetown, for example, although only a few miles apart on Bayside Road, roamed rather freely throughout upper Northampton County in early atlases.

Just as early maps provide a picture of what the Eastern Shore was like in pre-railroad days, so do written narratives. Many of the written records left by visitors are, predictably, accounts of visits to the barrier islands, usually for hunting and fishing trips. The Cobb family hotel opened just prior to the Civil War, and by 1870 or so was one of the most popular seaside resorts in the country. Accounts of visits to Cobbs Island were seen regularly in the outdoor press of the day. Alexander Hunter, a writer from Arlington, Virginia, was a regular hotel guest and wrote numerous stories about the seaside, many of

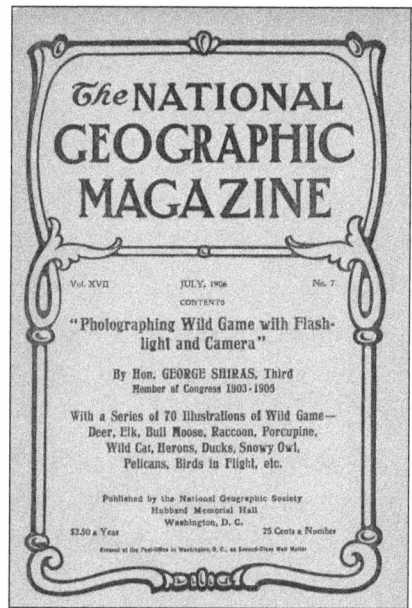

Alexander Hunter   National Geographic *cover*

which were included in his anthology *Huntsman in the South*, published in 1908. Other notable writers who covered the Shore include Rev. Thomas Dixon, who for a time lived in Cape Charles City and commuted by rail to a Baptist church in New York City, where he served as pastor. George Shiras was a congressman who championed some of America's first conservation legislation, and he had a home for nearly forty years on Revels Island. Shiras was a pioneering wildlife photographer, and his experiences on the Shore are chronicled in his two-volume set, *Hunting Wild Life With Camera and Flashlight*, published by the National Geographic Society.

Unfortunately, there are few written, descriptive accounts of visits to the *terra incognita* portion of the Eastern Shore prior to the opening of the railroad, and this leaves a void. Histories of the Eastern Shore are replete with dates and numbers and facts about land ownership, as well as laws passed and lawsuits filed and wills probated in the courts. These facts are important, of course, but they give little clue as to what people's lives were like, what they believed, what they did for fun,

English Customs Become American Ways

REVELS ISLAND CLUB ADJOINS THE "SWASH" CHANNEL
The author's cottage stands in the foreground. The large open fireplace in the living room invited many an oyster roast. On such occasions the attendant guides deftly opened these delicious bivalves for those grouped about the cheerful hearthstone. A well equipped dark room promptly recorded the results of each day's camera hunt. To the right are the cottage of another member and the main clubhouse.

Shiras Home

George Shiras wrote about Revels Island in his two-volume book Hunting Wild Life With Camera and Flashlight. *Shiras built this cottage on the island, and the photograph appears in his book. Shiras was the first photographer to have an entire issue of* National Geographic *devoted to his work. Pictured is the July 1906 issue with his photography.*

what their personalities were like. The reason for the void, naturally, is that few people set foot in *incognita land* other than permanent residents and their guests.

One who did was an artist from Wilmington, Delaware named Howard Pyle. A railroad linking the Shore with northern cities opened on April 7, 1876 when the Worcester Railroad christened a spur to Franklin City and thus gave birth to the great era of tourism on Chincoteague Island. Pyle was 23 and single at the time, an aspiring artist and writer who longed to escape his family's leather business in Wilmington. Pyle was educated at the Friends School and then studied art for three years with a Belgian artist named Van Der Weilen. When news broke of the railroad link to Chincoteague, Pyle sensed an opportunity for adventure and a chance to launch a career as a freelance writer and illustrator. That spring or early summer, Pyle bought a train ticket for Franklin City, took a steamer to Chincoteague, and booked a room at the brand-new Atlantic Hotel for a few weeks.

Pyle spent his time making sketches and interviewing local people as he explored the island. As a result, his article on Chincoteague was published in *Scribner's Monthly* in 1877, along with eleven of his sketches. Through *Scribner's*, Pyle introduced Chincoteague to an audience that had been largely unfamiliar with the coastal island. *Scribner's* was one of the most popular magazines in America at the time, and it's fair to say that Chincoteague's current status as a tourist destination began with a rail spur, a steamboat ride, and a talented and ambitious young writer and illustrator from Wilmington, Delaware.

Pyle successfully avoided the leather business, moved to New York City, and soon became one of the best-known illustrators in the country. Pyle is credited as a founder of the "Brandywine School" of painting, which includes the noted artist, Andrew Wyeth.

Encouraged by the success of his work on Chincoteague, Pyle expanded his range and in May 1879 published an article in *Harper's New Monthly Magazine* titled "A Peninsular Canaan," a sometimes fawning, sometimes acerbic look at what we today regard as the Delmarva Peninsula. Pyle describes the peninsula as a modern-day Canaan, a land of milk and honey, bypassed by modern times, clinging tenaciously to its old ways:

> One of the earliest English discoverers on this continent described the outlying Chesapeake shores of this peninsula, and its natural features have but little changed since that early time. When New York city was a wilderness inhabited by wild deer and Manhattoes, while Plymouth Rock all was still a virgin forest, Englishmen were growing tobacco, dredging oysters, and shooting wild fowl in this region. The vast tide of civilization has swept westward deluging the plains of Colorado southward to the chaparrals of Texas, and northward to the frozen shores

of Alaska, but has left the peninsula still clinging to old manners and customs, old modes of life and traditions with a firm tenacity. This is especially true the further southward one travels in this region, where, with but few exceptions, the descendants of the earlier settlers still live, with but a small increase of outside population. Separated from the outside world by the broad waters of the Delaware and Chesapeake, connected only by a narrow isthmus fifteen miles wide, with the body of the continent, one still finds here the easygoing old-time life, the broad hospitality of our forefathers, the careless air of ancient gentility, just tempered by an aristocratic exclusiveness. So the peninsula lies winking at the hurly-burly of modern progress, but it begins nevertheless at last to feel dubiously the intestine stir of modern Yankee notions in the midst of its indolent life.

For sixty-five miles of the lower length of the peninsula there is no railroad, and that in a country rich in natural products, easy of cultivation, and delightful in climate; there are but few steam saw or grist mills in a region abounding in valuable timber, and where corn meal is the staff of life; there are no steamboat lines on the Atlantic side, and but few on the Chesapeake, where almost the only means of being reached from the outside world is by water travel. Thus the southern peninsula, the garden spot of the country, to whose shore Nature seems to have invited man by every bounty she could lavish upon it, appears to be cut loose from the rest of the world, sleepily floating in the indolent sea of the past, incapable of crossing the gulf which separates it from outside modern life, and undesirous of joining in the race toward the wonderful future. *Requiescat in pace*, O Canaan of modern times, land overflowing with milk and honey, toward whose shores the footsteps of the pilgrim are directed *backward*! Who could visit thee and wish thee other than thou art?

While on the Eastern Shore of Virginia, Pyle visited Eastville, dined at the Eastville Inn, toured the office of the clerk of court, and then headed south to visit Custis Tomb at Arlington. He explored Hog Island, spending the night with a local family, and the next day witnessed an annual tradition on the island, the roundup and shearing of the sheep, which roamed freely over the island. He made numerous drawings during his visit, eleven of which were published in the magazine, along with those of other well-known illustrators such as A.B. Frost.

Pyle's narrative swings like a pendulum, at one extreme lush with praise and appreciation for the natural gifts of the Shore, and at the other dismissive and condescending of the people who hosted him. Pyle ends his piece with this paragraph:

> The poor are wofully (sic) ignorant, and as the upper classes are, in many instances, indolently unprogressive, though far less so than formerly. In short, the Virginia portion of the peninsula seems sunk in a Rip Van Winkle sleep that has lasted a hundred instead of twenty years, and that as yet shows but small signs of awakening.

Pyle was a young man when he visited, still in his twenties and eager to make an impression. His narration is engaging and his descriptions testify to his skill in the visual arts, but now and then it seems the hormones kick in and Pyle sets off on some sort of adolescent riff that urges the reader to pay attention to the writer rather than the subject at hand. My guess is that if Pyle had revisited the manuscript in middle age, he would have done some editing.

Yet, Pyle had a point. The English settled first on the southern tip of the peninsula and gradually moved north as more immigrants settled on the Eastern Shore. By the 1630s, communities along the bay in Maryland were being settled, many of which reflect their English heritage and their place names. The northern part of the peninsula became the focus of industry, principally shipbuilding, with Harlan and Hollingsworth of Wilmington one of the busiest in the young country. Pyle grew up in Wilmington and was raised in an atmosphere of ambition and industry. Growth was good. Progressive citizens worked together and everyone benefitted. Indolence was slothful, a negative force within the community. It held back progress.

The lower Eastern Shore was rural and sparsely populated, as was most of eastern Virginia in the 17th and 18th centuries. There was little industry, but there were trades, most of which centered on either farming or fishing. Most settlers came from England and many were involved in indenture situations where they agreed to work for a skilled craftsman for a period of time in exchange for room, board, clothing, and instruction in a particular line of work. Historian Susie M. Ames called indenture "the original on-the-job training program in America."

For immigrants who could not afford passage from England to America, indentured servitude made the journey possible and also ensured work and shelter upon arrival in the new country. Many of the servants were indentured to planters. Sometimes indenture was made by the father on behalf of a son. Ames, in her book *Studies of the Virginia Eastern Shore in the Seventeenth Century*, gave the example of James Lee and Peter Pritchard of Accomack regarding Pritchard's son, Joseph, who wanted to learn the trade of tailor. Joseph Pritchard agreed to serve Lee for four years and three months in order to learn the trade. Lee would provide food, clothing, and shelter to Joseph during the period of indenture and give Lee some tools of the trade when the indenture ended.

In 1696, arrangements were made for Reginald Eyre, the eldest son of Benjamin and Martha Eyre, to live with Thomas Bonewell to learn the trade of a blacksmith. John Sharpley of Accomack County bound his son John to George Key, shoemaker, "the said Key to instruct John Sharpley in the art and trade of shoe making or cordwinder." Indentures were legal agreements and were recorded in court orders in both counties.

Slavery was once considered the ugly domain of the great plantations of the South, where blood was spilled in the land of mint juleps to prop up King Cotton. Slavery was much more common than once thought, and even on the Eastern Shore, generally considered rural and poor, most farms had at least a few slaves. James Mears wrote in *Hacks Neck and Its People – Both Past and Present*, that slavery existed in Hacks Neck from colonial times through the Civil War. Slaves were often sold during Saturday afternoon social gatherings in Pungoteague, according to Mears.

Advances in genealogical research, including access to vast

databases such as census information and wills, are showing just how common slavery was. Those of us who thought of slavery as being restricted to the plantation class, that our ancestors were poor farmers and landowners who were somehow above the ugliness of slavery, had better think again. If your great-great-grandaddy was a farmer, he was likely a slave owner.

I had never given the issue much thought and assumed that my ancestors were small farmers who raised large families in order to get the work done, but then I went on the new MilesFiles genealogical database of the Eastern Shore Heritage Center, and found that a lot of my people spent their Saturday afternoons hanging out in Pungoteague. And they weren't there to eat peanuts and drink root beer.

My farming family in the years prior to the Civil War owned, at one time or another, from five to fourteen other people. Owned them. Let that sink in.

Strangely, I did not feel sadness about this, or guilt. It was something that happened. And I know that you cannot defend evil by saying that everyone was doing it, ...but everyone was doing it.

I do not have plantations in my pedigree. My great-great-granddaddy walked behind a mule. But he had a slave walking alongside him dropping seed potatoes into the furrow. That is just the way it was. He farmed less than a hundred acres, but for a man and a mule, that is a lot of land. He needed help. He went to Pungoteague to find it.

Small farmers needed labor just as surely as the plantations did, although on a smaller scale. Many farmers had a few slaves, and most of them lived under the same roof as the farming family, worked together, and shared meals.

Perhaps the acceptance of indenture as a moral issue could have been rationalized and extended to slavery. The indentured and the slaves lived similar lives. Both were given food, clothing, shelter, and medical care. The indentured servant worked under a legal contract that specified an end date of the indenture, at which time the servant would be released from the obligation and given a reward of some sort that had been previously agreed upon, often a cow, a barrel of corn, or a new suit of clothes. The slave had no contract, and there was no end date. There was no reward. The slave was property. Indentures were part of a structured training process.

Indentures were not restricted to the working classes. "Since apprenticeship was about the only means of securing industrial training at that time, it was sometimes sought by individuals fairly fortunate as regards birth and material possessions," wrote Ames.

Consider the case of the Parramores, one of the more noted families of the Eastern Shore who owned a plantation called *Bellevue* on the seaside southeast of Accomac. The Parramores fought in the American Revolution and later served the community as judges, doctors, and elected officials. The first Parramore came to America as an indentured servant, but by the time of the Revolution the family was among the leaders of the growing Virginia colony.

John Parramore arrived in 1622 aboard the *Bona Venture* as a 17-year-old servant to John Blower. By the 1630s Parramore's name was appearing regularly in court documents, ranging in nature from litigation over business transactions to a charge of cursing on the Sabbath. By the early 1640s, Parramore was thriving to the point where he had an indentured servant of his own, Edward Robins.

Many descriptions of the Eastern Shore in the pre-railroad days depict the peninsula as rural and poor. The necks were decidedly rural, but to describe the people as poor begs the question, "relative to what?" Howard Pyle on one hand describes the landscape as verdant and lush, providing a bounty from both land and sea. Yet the people are woefully ignorant, indolent, and unprogressive.

The people of the necks lived closely with the land and the sea and by some standards could be described as poor, if your definition of the term involves bank balances and investment portfolios. They could be described as ignorant if a measure of knowledge involves Greek classics. They could be unprogressive if progressive means being unsatisfied with your current lot in life and in constant need of something newer and better.

The Upshurs and a Life of Service

About 1637 Arthur Upshur, a boy of twelve, came to Virginia from Essex County, England. Perhaps his original home was Colchester or one of the nearby towns of Coggeshall, Bocking, Dedham or Wormingford where Upchers were living at that time. Upon his arrival in Virginia Arthur went to the "Plantacon of Acchawmacke" on the Eastern Shore where he established his home in the New World.

With those three simple, elegant sentences John Andrews Upshur begins his narrative of one of the Eastern Shore's most gifted and influential families. Arthur Upshur, a boy of twelve, left behind an unknown past in a village in the English countryside and came to America where he begat a family that would not only become prominent in Northampton and Accomack Counties, but would serve presidents, become military leaders, and represent their home and country at the highest levels.

John Upshur published his book, *Upshur Family in Virginia*, in 1953, likely influenced by a family friend, Ralph T. Whitelaw, whose two-volume history, *Virginia's Eastern Shore*, had come out two years earlier. In 1927 Ralph and his wife Paula bought the plantation Warwick, near Quinby, and restored it. Warwick was the home of Arthur Upshur, who is buried on the grounds, along with many other members of the Upshur family.

While Whitelaw's book is an exhaustive documentary of land grants, patents, property transfers, architecture, and history of the Eastern Shore, Upshur's book zeros in on one family – the Upchurs,

Upshotts, or Upshurs – the latter spelling having been generally accepted by the family. Upshur's book – a combination history and genealogy – documents the indelible influence a 12-year-old boy from a village in Essex had on the Eastern Shore.

Little is known of Arthur Upshur's life in England. According to some accounts, Arthur booked passage to the colonies to escape the clutches of a vicious step-mother. Neither is it known how he arrived in the New World. He could have come by way of Holland, the West Indies, New Netherlands, or New England. Considerable trade was going on between the Eastern Shore and those parts of the world, and it was not uncommon for new settlers to be part of the cargo.

The Upshurs were apparently commoners back in England – planters, fishermen, or shopkeepers, perhaps – but on the Eastern Shore they were as close to an upper class as we will find. The Upshurs owned a great deal of land, they were educated, and they believed in service to country. The Upshurs were very much a part of the order of social aristocracy created by living independently on a remote peninsula for many years, with marriage and remarriage linking many generations of leading families. As John Upshur commented, "...it is difficult to write a genealogy of one without writing a genealogy of all."

The story of the Upshur family is reminiscent of that of the Kennedys of Massachusetts. An immigrant arrives as a young man, finds wealth and status in the New World, and sires a large family that is committed to community and public service. The family prospers and has admirers far and wide, but at the same time is beset by tragedy and misfortune. The story begins with Arthur Upshur.

How to be a Success in the New World

The modern generation of Upshurs have been among the Eastern Shore's most accomplished genealogists and historians. Through their skills, we can look back at the lives of ancestors such as Arthur Upshur and get a better understanding of what was required to survive an ocean voyage as a child, to follow that with indentured servitude, and finally to become a successful merchant, plantation owner, and community leader.

Genealogy is for many of us a tedious occupation, a collection of names, dates, and places, a spreadsheet of Old Testament accounts of who begat whom. But now and then, when genealogy is done skillfully and thoroughly, a story emerges from the spreadsheets that brings context and life to the names and dates. Such is the case of Arthur Upshur and the remarkable family he sired.

Arthur Upshur could have written a how-to book on finding success and fortune in the New World. If he did, his formula would go like this:

Marry young.
Marry often.
Marry well.

Arthur used this approach to create an Upshur dynasty that stretched from Occohannock Neck to Church Neck and Cedar Grove on the bayside, and on the seaside from Brownsville, near Nassawadox, north through Upshur Neck, all the way to Rose Cottage on Finneys Creek in Accomack County. Of course, Arthur did not leave us a how-to book on finding success in the New World. According to his biographer, Arthur could neither read nor write, but he possessed an uncanny acumen for doing business, wonderful negotiating skills, and a knack for being in the right place at the right time. He taught by example.

Arthur's adventure began when he was 12 years old and boarded a sailing vessel for the New World. Family history holds that Arthur was in the company of an older brother, Abel, and the two reached the Virginia Capes in 1637. Upon landing, Abel reportedly made his way to Gloucester County on the western shore of the bay, but court records there were destroyed in a fire in 1820 and no paper trail remains to document the life of Abel in Gloucester.

Arthur came to the Eastern Shore and was indentured to Captain William Stone for a period of about a year, long enough to satisfy the fee for passage from England, and his name was entered in court records dated January 11, 1641 among the headrights listed by Capt. Stone in his application for a land patent. This is the first documented presence of Arthur Upshur in Virginia, although he was likely here for some time before that.

The big unknown is why Arthur and his brother Abel left Essex County and sailed for America. Many immigrants were arriving for religious reasons. During the period of the Upshurs' arrival a group of early dissenters left the Essex township of Dedham in 1635 to found a community of the same name in the Massachusetts Bay Colony. Under the leadership of John Rogers, a preacher banned from his work in England, they established a settlement on the western edge of the colony that today is a suburb of Boston. It is possible that Abel and Arthur made their way to Virginia by passing through the Massachussetts Bay Colony, accompanying a group of religious dissenters who were their neighbors in East Anglia.

It is likely that the two Upshur boys were sent on their voyage by their family, rather than setting sail on their own volition. It is likely also that their parents knew Capt. Stone, or at least knew of him, and were confident that the brothers would be cared for when they reached American soil. Indeed, Arthur's indenture with Capt. Stone seems to have gone well. Capt. Stone lived on a plantation he had inherited from his father between Hungars and Mattawoman Creeks in an area now known as Wilsonia Neck. Capt. Stone was a prominent person in Northampton and has the distinction of being the county's first sheriff. Jennings C. Wise, in his 1911 history of the Eastern Shore, *Ye Kingdome of Accawmacke*, takes that distinction a notch higher by declaring Stone "America's first sheriff."

According to Wise, Stone was recruited by Lord Baltimore to encourage settlers in Virginia to invest in land in Maryland, and he successfully persuaded Edmund Scarburgh, John Custis, and Francis Yeardley, among others, to do so. For his efforts, Stone was commissioned governor of Maryland. In 1653 he took his own advice, sold his property on Hungars Creek to William Whittington, and moved up the Potomac to Charles County, Maryland, where he died in 1695. One of his descendants was Thomas Stone, a signer of the Declaration of Independence, whose home at Port Tobacco is a National Historic Site. Thomas Stone purchased his 442-acre plantation from Daniel Jenifer, his uncle, who was prominently featured in the Edmund Scarburgh - Anne Toft - Daniel Jenifer triangle. (See "Sex and Violence in Gargathy Neck")

By the mid-17th century, the mechanics of immigration, indenture, and compensation in acres paid had become a predictable system with many familiar names turning up at regular intervals. Between 1640 and 1660, 40,000 people immigrated to America from England, so the system had been in place and working for some time. Some, of course, worked the system better than others. Edmund Scarburgh and his family dominated during the early days, along with his protégé Mrs. Anne Toft. And Arthur Upshur was the pioneer of a second wave of familial domination that accounted for thousands of acres of land, mainly in Northampton County.

On October 28, 1651 Arthur became a landowner for the first time when he was awarded a patent for 300 acres at the head of Occohannock Creek as compensation for transporting to Virginia six immigrants from England. Arthur married during this period, and it is known that he had two sons, but the name of his first wife is not known. She must have died prior to 1655, because in that year Arthur married Mary Risden, widow of Phillip Risden, formerly of London. Arthur's marriage to the Widow Risden is the first which has documented proof. On May 7, 1655 he applied to the court for letters of administration on the estate of Mr. Risden, "lately deceased," whose widow he had married.

Arthur gained 300 more acres in Occohannock Neck in 1656 for transporting to Virginia six more immigrants from England, some of whom were his wife's relatives. A third patent in 1661 for 100 acres was added to his holdings, giving him an impressive spread of 700 acres. His biographer, John Upshur, estimates that Arthur and Mary lived at Occohannock for about 13 years, raising four children there, and possibly more. According to court records, Arthur added numerous improvements to his property, creating a substantial plantation.

Mary died about 1662 and in 1663 Arthur married Mary Hammond-Jacob, possibly the daughter of Dr. George Clarke of Northampton County. Arthur was Mary's third husband, following Mark Hammond, and then Richard Jacob. She was Arthur's third wife. Through this marriage, Arthur became the owner of Cedar Grove, a large plantation near Hungars Church east of Bridgetown.

So, since arriving in Virginia around 1637 as a 12-year-old boy, by the time he was a young man in his mid-thirties, Arthur had established a plantation of 700 acres at the head of Occohannock Creek, and he also became owner of the Cedar Grove plantation through his marriage to Mary Hammond-Jacob, who had inherited the property. But more was yet to come.

Arthur and Mary moved from Occohannock to Cedar Grove, and Arthur sold much of the Occohannock property to his step-sons, keeping for himself a tract where a mill was in operation. In 1664 Arthur patented 200 acres in what would become known as Upshur Neck, on the seaside between Hog Island Bay and Machipongo River. Shortly thereafter. he purchased the remainder of the neck of land from Colonel William Kendall for 16,000 pounds of tobacco.

Around 1678 Arthur and Mary moved from Cedar Grove and built a home in the northern part of Upshur Neck in an area known as Warwick, which would become the ancestral home of the Upshur family, just south of the present village of Quinby. Arthur gave 1,000 acres on the southern portion of the neck to his son, Arthur II, who built a home at what was known as Essex, or Point Farm. Just across the creek from Point Farm lived the Brown family, whose daughter, Sarah, caught the eye of Arthur Jr. In 1690 they were married, and thus the plantation Brownsville joined the Upshur family holdings. When Sarah's father died in 1708, the Upshurs inherited the property.

Arthur lived to be 85, and when he passed away in 1709, family assets included land at Occohannock, Cedar Grove, Warwick, and Brownsville. Later, a fourth generation Upshur would add to the portfolio the contemporary showplace of the Upshur family, Vaucluse in Church Neck. The Upshur family had owned land in Church Neck since 1768, when Arthur Upshur IV bought about 550 acres on the shores of Hungars Creek from the estate of William Waters. Littleton Upshur (1758-1811), the son of Arthur IV, was born and raised at Warwick, and when he was 21 he inherited the 550 acre tract from his father. He married Ann Parker (1763-1820) and the two of them built Vaucluse and raised nine children there. Vaucluse was considered one of the outstanding architectural and cultural centers of the Eastern Shore.

Vaucluse

While Warwick is considered the ancestral home of the Upshur family – their American sire is buried there – it is Vaucluse that projects the energy, style, and progressive image of the Upshurs, who were gentlemen, statesmen, and leaders during the 19th century at both state and national levels. Vaucluse was built by Littleton and Ann Parker Upshur, who were a vibrant, educated, energetic couple with many friends not only on the Eastern Shore, but around the state and region.

Littleton and Ann had nine children, and the home on Hungars Creek grew as the family did. According to Whitelaw's history, the oldest part of the mansion is the section with the brick end and two fireplaces, which was built around 1784 by Littleton and Ann Upshur. Other sections were added as the need arose, and were the work of subsequent owners, including Judge Abel Upshur, a son of Littleton and Ann, and later by the Wilkins and Pope families.

Vaucluse was a showplace known and admired by many around the state, and it became symbolic of the Eastern Shore's landed gentry, which was more readily manifest in Northampton than in Accomack. Indeed, the 18th and 19th centuries were something of a period of refinement and elegance, a mingling of English manners with new American wealth and opportunity. People of the Eastern Shore were involved not only in commerce and business, but in serving the community, the commonwealth, and the nation. That is not to say there were no scalawags or jackasses, but the people of the Eastern Shore generally lived well and served the community, as witnessed by artifacts and architecture surviving from the period.

The lives of the Upshurs and their contemporaries disprove the notion suggested by Howard Pyle and others that the necks of the Eastern Shore were populated by ignorant, indolent, slothful persons whose remote existence had spawned generations of interbred and passive souls who knew not and cared not what lay beyond the limits of their vision.

As previously stated, the Eastern Shore necks and their neighboring waterways formed an avenue of commerce and communication that was lacking farther inland, where wagon trails and stage coaches offered limited options for doing business and visiting kinfolk. The Upshurs were significant landowners, and they and other families of similar means were in a position to live well on income provided by the property they owned. This allowed some the luxury of public service, whether via politics, the church, or through military service.

In 1907 Georgiana Tankard Fitzhugh of Sylvan Scene in Northampton County published *The Life of Dr. John Tankard*, her grandfather, who was born in 1758 and died in 1836. In a chapter of "miscellaneous comments" Mrs. Fitzhugh writes of society in Northampton County during the time period of her grandfather's life:

> At this time Hon. Abel P. Upshur was Circuit Judge and resided at Vaucluse, in Northampton Co. Gen. Severn E. Parker was perhaps the most distinguished and eloquent lawyer at the bar. Mr. John Eyre the wealthiest man, and excelled by none in refinement, elegance, and all the qualities of mind and heart, that go to make up a gentleman, in the truest sense of the word. He was the acknowledged leader of a society, that numbered among its members, some of the most intelligent, courtly and agreeable men and women, who ever graced any circle. Not a few of them could trace their descent to the nobility of England. They have left to their descendants, an inheritance of virtue and honor. Even so lately as the time of the civil war, the soldiers

from Northampton, were remarkable for their courtesy, and politeness.

The Upshur family, and Vaucluse, were known throughout the state. Upon the death of Littleton Upshur in 1811, the *Richmond Enquirer* published this letter:

> Before this reaches you, the newspapers will have informed you of the death of our esteemed friend Littleton Upshur, Ltd. ...The Eastern Shore of Virginia will long mourn the loss of one of her noblest sons. There are but few upon this side of the Bay who knew his worth better than myself. He was an upright, just and honest man – liberal and benevolent. I will leave it to a stronger pen than mine to portray the character of this worthy man.
>
> But, my friend, what shall I say of Vaucluse – will you go with me to visit and soothe the feelings of this most amiable family; come then and let us away – we will advise them not to grieve overmuch – that tho' his race was short (about 55 years of age) it was glorious – and that he is gone to the command of his Heavenly Father to join his family above – that by his attention, his care, and his superior judgement he had left them everything wherewith to be comforted.
>
> I shall feel extremely gratified in visiting with you once more that seat of happiness where nature and art so effectually combine to banish melancholy, and to drive our sorrows away.

Littleton and Ann Parker Upshur raised a very notable family. Of their nine children, some prospered and found success on a national stage, but there also was great tragedy in their family. It was a Kennedy-esque mixture of lofty highs, tempered by sudden, unpredictable violence. There was the gift of love, and the heartbreak of having it taken away.

Littleton and Ann's firstborn was a son, Littleton II, who had a very successful career in state politics, serving in both the Senate and House of Delegates. He was a captain in the 27th Regiment of Virginia Militia for Northampton County during the War of 1812, and members of his regiment included several of his younger brothers. Arthur, born in 1788, was an ensign in the regiment. Younger brothers John (b.

1792) and George (b. 1799) were both privates. Throughout his adult life, Littleton was called Colonel Upshur.

Their oldest daughter, Juliet (b. 1784) married John T. Elliott, a merchant of Franktown who was a business partner of John Upshur of Brownsville. Her younger sister, Leah Custis (b. 1797) married Peter Mayo, a successful businessman from Norfolk. Elizabeth (b 1801), the youngest of the nine, married local businessman John E. Nottingham, with whom she had two sons and one daughter.

One of the most promising of their sons, John, was the first in their family to face tragedy. Born at Vaucluse in 1792, John studied medicine and established a practice on the Eastern Shore. On April 15, 1818, John married 22-year-old Lucy Parker. Just two weeks after the wedding, Lucy died suddenly. John was devastated and heartbroken. Eighteen days after the death of his bride, John took his own life. The couple were buried together at Sylvan Retreat, now known as the Bull Farm, near Pungoteague.

Military service played a role in many of the lives of the Upshur men, perhaps a result of their youthful involvement in their big brother's 27th Regiment of Virginia during the War of 1812. Commander George Parker Upshur (b. 1799) entered the Navy as a midshipman in 1818 and spent his career in uniform. George married Margaret Eyre Parker of Selma, near Eastville, in 1836 and purchased a farm in Old Town Neck he called Caserta, after a village in Italy he had visited while in the navy. George apparently intended to enlarge the home on the farm and use it when the time came to end his military career, but tragedy also befell his family. An infant son died, followed shortly by his young wife, and then their 2-year-old daughter. Commander Upshur lost interest in Caserta and sold the property in 1847.

After the family tragedy, Commander Upshur sought solace in his navy career. In 1843-44 he commanded the *U.S.S. Truston* on her first cruise to the Mediterranean, and in 1847 was named Superintendent of the U.S. Naval Academy at Annapolis, only the second officer to hold that position. In 1852 he took command of the *U.S.S. Levant* in Norfolk and joined the Mediterranean Squadron. He died while on board in

Spezia, Italy. His body was returned to the Eastern Shore where he was buried at Vaucluse beside his wife and their two children.

Perhaps the best known of the Vaucluse Upshurs was the sixth son of Littleton and Ann, Abel Parker Upshur, who was, in the words of Ralph Whitelaw, "...one of the Shore's most distinguished sons and held many important local, state, and national offices, all with great credit to himself."

Abel Upshur was born at Vaucluse on June 17, 1790. He studied law, was admitted to the bar in 1810, and practiced law in Richmond for several years. In 1824 he returned to his homeplace and that year was elected to the General Assembly. In 1826 he was appointed a judge of the Circuit Court in Williamsburg. While living in Williamsburg, Abel purchased Bassett Hall and lived there while attending to court business. It is said that Vice-President Tyler was visiting with Abel in 1841 when word came of the death of President Harrison. When President Tyler was inaugurated, he asked Abel to come to Washington to serve as Secretary of the Navy. Abel held that position for two years, and then received a cabinet appointment when he succeeded Daniel Webster as Secretary of State. Abel Upshur, a native of Church Neck, became the only Eastern Shoreman to have served in a presidential cabinet.

Abel's political career ended tragically in 1844 when he was killed in an explosion aboard a ship when a cannon was being unveiled to the news media and the public. The incident took place on February 28 aboard the *U.S.S. Princeton* on the Potomac River. A cannon had been developed that was many times more powerful than any in current use anywhere in the world, and it was hoped that this show of strength would act as a deterrent to any possible aggressors. Hence, the new cannon was called "The Peacemaker." The 12-inch cannon weighed 27,000 pounds, and in 1844 it was the most powerful weapon on Earth. The cannon was capable of such destruction its makers believed it would never see the violence of war, but instead be a great deterrent. No nation would ever be so foolhardy as to challenge a country with such a formidable weapon in its arsenal.

The Upshurs and a Life of Service

A new steam frigate named the *U.S.S. Princeton* had just been launched on the Potomac River, and she was armed with a pair of cannons, one for the starboard side and one for the port. On February 28, 1844 the *Princeton* and her pair of Peacemakers would be introduced to the American public.

The frigate was launched with appropriate pomp and ceremony. Bands played as 400 invited guests boarded the *Princeton* to witness a history-making event, the first firing of the great cannons from a steamship. On board were President John Tyler, Secretary of War William Wilkins, and a former First Lady, 75-year-old Dolley Madison. Tens of thousands lined the banks of the Potomac to watch.

Also among the dignitaries was Abel Upshur, the Secretary of State from the Eastern Shore. In the weeks preceding the *Princeton's* launch, Abel Upshur's days had been filled with negotiations for the annexation of Texas. Legislation looked promising, and while annexation was backed by most Americans, it was opposed by the Mexican government, which considered Texas a province in revolt. Should Mexico consider forcing the issue, the presence of the *Princeton* in the Gulf of Mexico might bring second thoughts.

But on an unseasonably warm day in late February, the *Princeton* and her Peacemakers would become the focus of what newspapers of the day called the worse peacetime tragedy in history. The cannons were fired two times with impressive success, but news accounts say officials decided to fire a third round as the *Princeton* neared Mount Vernon, as a salute to the nation's first president. This time, the cannon failed, and the explosion sent flames and shrapnel ripping through the cabin of the frigate. Secretary Upshur was killed instantly, as was Navy Secretary Thomas Gilmer and wealthy New York banker David Gardiner, among others. The president was below decks at the time of the explosion and narrowly escaped death.

Abel Upshur, who had grown up one of nine children of Littleton and Ann Upshur, was buried with honors in Oak Hill Cemetery in Washington, one of the few Upshurs not to have been buried at the ancestral home Warwick, in Upshur Neck, or at the family cemetery at

Abel Upshur

Vaucluse, where most of Abel's brothers and sisters were laid to rest.

Abel Upshur left his entire estate to his wife and their daughter, Susan, who was their only surviving child. Abel's wife, Elizabeth Brown Upshur, was the daughter of John Brown Upshur and his wife, Mary Elizabeth, who owned Rose Cottage on Finneys Creek.

After Abel's death, Vaucluse changed hands several times and was owned by the Dunton, Nottingham, and Wilkins families over the years. The 550 acres once owned by Abel Upshur have long since been divided, and much of the property today is a housing development called "Vaucluse Shores."

The Upshurs and Ralph T. Whitelaw

In early 1951 Ralph T. Whitelaw's *Virginia's Eastern Shore* hit the bookstores. The handsome two-volume set was bound in black cloth and decorated with gilding. It was an exhaustive chronicle of land transfers, patents, and descriptions of the homes of people who populated the Shore during the first two centuries of English settlement. The set included 1,511 pages and weighed in at nine pounds. It sold for a princely (for 1951) $17.50.

Today a mint set of the 1951 Whitelaw history would hover in the $1,000 range; even a less desirable 1968 printing in "fair" condition was offered recently for $300.

The story of Ralph T. Whitelaw and his obsession with his adopted community is like a passion play that ends with a heroic effort muted by tragedy.

The Upshurs and a Life of Service

Whitelaw was born in St. Louis, Missouri, in September 1880, a member of a prominent family that operated a chemical business for generations. Ralph attended Amherst College, received a degree in chemical engineering, and went to work in the family business. In 1917, at age 37, he became president of the company.

Ralph served overseas during World War I, and then returned to St. Louis and married Paula Oertel on April 1, 1922. Ralph settled into the business and social world of St. Louis and was described in a centennial history of the state of Missouri as "very active in support of all movements for the advancement and welfare of the city."

Surprisingly, Ralph and Paula took an early retirement in 1926 when Ralph was just 46. The couple traveled the country for several months, looking for a pleasant region to begin a life of retirement. The couple discovered the Eastern Shore and soon began a new chapter in their lives.

Ralph always had an interest in history and architecture and the Whitelaws discovered an old home for sale near the village of Quinby. The home was called Warwick and had been in the Upshur family for generations. There was a story that the home had been partially burned in a British raid during the Revolution, and that piqued Ralph's interest. The cottage was in bad shape. It had been lived in by a stream of tenants who had been indifferent to upkeep, and the Whitelaws decided to buy the cottage and give it a new life.

The couple moved to Accomac, began working part time restoring Warwick, and started a real estate business called simply Whitelaw and Whitelaw. The real estate business introduced Ralph to some of the architectural wonders hidden down back roads and wooded necks. He began photographing and documenting these properties and researching early land patents and transactions.

Meanwhile, as the Whitelaws went about the deliberate process of reviving Warwick, they developed a close relationship with the Upshur family, whose ancestors were buried on the plantation. Anne Floyd Upshur was about Ralph's age and shared his interest in documenting land ownership and the evolution of architectural styles on the Shore.

Warwick Plantation

Her father was Thomas Teackle Upshur, II, a highly respected historian and genealogist who had restored many of the court records of Northampton County. The Upshurs lived at Brownsville, just south of Upshur Neck, a plantation that Arthur Upshur II and his wife Sarah inherited in 1708 when her father died.

Around 1928 Ralph and Paula moved into Warwick, which one newspaper account described as "a charming and most livable home." Ralph divided his time between selling real estate, studying property transfers and ancient land patents, and involving himself with the Chamber of Commerce, the Association for the Preservation of Virginia Antiquities, and other community organizations.

Tragically, Paula Whitelaw died in 1933, and after her passing Ralph seemed to lose interest in maintaining Warwick. Ralph moved to Accomac, built a cottage near the Whispering Pines motor lodge, and there he spent the remainder of his life.

The Upshurs and a Life of Service

From around 1935 until his death in 1950 Ralph dedicated himself to compiling property records and historic documents from both counties, with the intention of publishing them in a book. He, with the help of Anne Upshur, collected information on more than 200 Eastern Shore buildings of the 17th, 18th, and early 19th centuries.

Ralph became ill in 1949, but worked on the book until he had assembled all the text and was ready to deliver it to his publisher, the Virginia Historical Society. Tragically, Ralph passed away before his book would go to press. The only task that remained was to compile an index, and this was done by his friend George Carrington Mason of the historical society.

Ralph T. Whitelaw died on Sunday, March 26, 1950 at Northampton-Accomack Memorial Hospital. A memorial service was conducted the following day by Rev. Edwin T. Williams at St. James Episcopal Church in Accomac. In accordance with his wishes, his remains were cremated and his ashes placed next to those of Paula Whitelaw at Ferncliff Cemetery in Ardsley, New York.

Virginia's Eastern Shore – A History of Northampton and Accomack Counties was a monumental work, and more than 70 years after publication is still sought after and respected. The project was heroic in scope, an effort of thorough dedication, and yet it ended in tragedy. The book consumed more than 15 years of the author's life. And yet he never got to hold a copy in his hands.

Essex, the Upshurs, and the Eastern Shore

The Upshurs were from Essex, a county northeast of London, perhaps best known today as a commuter hub for folks working in the city. This is true for the portions of Essex close by the capital, but as one travels farther north and east, the landscape of the county changes. Commuter communities give way to open country, to farms, woodland, and small villages, many of which are on the coast, or along picturesque landscapes such as the Stour River valley. The farther you remove yourself from London, the more Essex resembles the Eastern Shore.

Brochures promoting tourism in Essex claim that the county suffers from its proximity to London, that it offers far more than a tapestry of bedroom communities for London's office workers. The Essex coastline "has broad sandy beaches and remote salt marshes are still off the beaten path and often crowd-free."

Broad sandy beaches and remote salt marshes off the beaten path, and just a few hours travel from the nation's capital and the financial hub of the country. Imagine that.

By the time Arthur Upshur sailed from Essex to the Eastern Shore, he likely had a good idea what he was getting into, as did his family. No one knows exactly which town in Essex the Upshurs called home. It could have been Dedham, where religious dissenters were beginning to immigrate to the Massachusetts colony to seek freedom to worship as they wished. It could have been Wivenhoe, a fishing village on an estuary of the North Sea where life revolved around the winds and the tides and the seasonal migration of fish. Or it could have been Mersea Island, where growing and consuming oysters was a 2,000-year-old tradition.

By the year 1637 a system was well in place where immigrants could come to Virginia, have their travel expenses covered by a sponsor, and agree to work for the sponsor for a specified time, often learning a trade during that period, and being provided room and board as well. The officials of the colony actively recruited young men and women to come to James City and begin a new life. Arthur Upshur, if he happened to hail from one of the coastal regions of Essex, would have been at home on the Eastern Shore, amid the broad sandy beaches and remote salt marshes. Arthur worked as indentured servant for William Stone, who owned land on the Chesapeake Bay in what is now Wilsonia Neck. Once Arthur's indenture was satisfied, he became a free man and soon was a landowner himself.

Arthur chose for his first land holding 300 acres at the headwaters of Occohannock Creek, not far from the plantation where he served his indenture. It was a remote area of forest, marshland, and tidal waterways, likely very similar to the landscape of his native Essex. There seems to exist a kinship between Essex and the Eastern Shore that lingers today, and it manifests itself in varied ways. One of England's most popular contemporary sculptors lives in the village of Wivenhoe, but his work is inspired and infomed by the Virginia coast, especially the tidal flats of the seaside and the magical edge where land meets sea. It could be said that the coast of Virginia is a mirror image of the coast of England's Essex.

Guy Taplin's Life at the Edge

Guy Taplin lives in a former sea captain's cottage in Wivenhoe and he has a woodworking shop in the garden shed, but he spends most of his creative time in a rambling beach cottage on the Colne estuary near the North Sea. It is the life of a hermit, and Guy's seaside compound appears to be the work of a nautical packrat, a rambling collection of flotsam and castoffs, all of it gifts of the sea. Guy can be seen on a gray hazy day, walking the beach with head bowed, foraging for found objects to be given a new life – perhaps, someday.

Guy lives on the coast of England, but his work is grounded in the coast of Virginia, both rural, remote areas where for generations human lives have been intertwined with the landscape that is home. The similarities shared by Wivenhoe and the Eastern Shore are remarkable. A brief online history of the town says that its good fortune was a product of the railroad, which opened in 1873 and made the markets of London easily accessible for Essex seafood. The rail also stimulated the boat-building business in Wivenhoe by making raw materials available.

When Guy visited America for the first time, he went to Chincoteague, which he considered heaven on earth. "There's nothing I like better than getting on a beach that's full of driftwood, or finding a seaport that still has some of its integrity left and is still a working port," he said.

But the highlight of Guy's visit to America was the Virginia barrier islands, specifically Cobbs Island, where from about 1840 to 1896 the

Cobb family operated one of the best-known hotels on the Atlantic coast. It was a rustic collection of cabins and rambling dormitories and dining halls, a place favored by beachgoers in the summer and duck hunters in the winter. The Cobbs supplemented their resort income with a wrecking business, salvaging ships that grounded on their island shoals for a percentage of the cargo.

Guy Taplin

Guy would have fit right in with the Cobbs on their remote island, sharing the magic of finding something of value washed up by the sea, a serendipitous gift of the storm gods. The challenge of the storm gods was that the finder was charged with discovering what to do with that gift to give it value. For the Cobbs it often involved making duck decoys to use in their hunting business. Nathan Cobb, Jr., the first son of the founder, was especially adept at finding the likeness of birds in a collection of flotsam that might include a shattered ship mast that would be shaped into a duck's body, the gnarly base of a cedar tree that would yield a head, or the bleached limb of a holly that miraculously resembled a greater yellowlegs shorebird.

The Cobbs had a gift of using the most rudimentary materials to capture the essence of a bird. They developed this talent out of necessity, because on a remote island in the decade following the Civil War there were no power tools to produce detail that would make a bird appear realistic. So they did it by closely watching birds – their postures and movements – and then using a hatchet and knife to capture the essence of the bird with minimal detail. They realized that it is not the texture of feathers that makes the bird appear alive, but its movement, its body language.

And this is what Guy learned from the Cobbs, from closely studying their work, and from emulating not only their technique, but their ethos, their need to use found objects for unintended purposes. *The Financial Times of London* described a Taplin exhibition this way: "Visitors to the exhibition who have not yet discovered his magic way with wood can see for themselves how, with the simplest possible shape and outline, he seems to encapsulate the spirit of the bird he has in mind. He seems to be able to do with a bold shape and some simple paint what Matisse could do with a few strokes."

Guy does not attempt to carve birds that look like they may have come from the hands of Nathan Cobb. Rather, it is the spirit of the bird, the way it is produced, that is important. "It's not a matter of getting ideas from old carvings, but they serve as a bedrock, almost a family," he said in an interview with *Wildfowl Carving and Collecting* magazine. "I remember (Virginia carver) Pete Peterson saying he could stand at his door and hear the surf on Cobbs Island. Well, so can I, when I'm at my shop on the coast. I'm just an ocean away. It's a communion that goes on, like the Cobbs are part of my family. I can understand, in religion, believers needing external symbols – a cross or something tangible – to make the transition between the real and the spiritual. The carved bird is the symbol of the coast. It means more than simply a tool of the hunt."

Planters, Mariners, and Merchants

The first industry on the Eastern Shore was salt-making. Salt was needed to preserve fish and other foods for times when things were scarce. During the first years of the Jamestown Colony, many people died of starvation and disease. The colony turned to the Eastern Shore for the precious crystals that would help them survive a winter.

Salt was made by heating sea water until the liquid was vaporized, leaving a crusty layer of crystals. The colony sent a small group of men to the tip of the Eastern Shore peninsula, where they set up salt making facilities on Smith and Mockhorn Islands. The sea water was sometimes heated in large vats with a fire built below, and salt was also derived from the simple process of evaporation by the sun. The men lived on the mainland in an encampment called Dale's Gift, where they also grew corn, squash, and other vegetables for the Jamestown settlement.

Dale's Gift was the creation of acting governor Sir Thomas Dale, and theories vary as to its exact location, and to the origin of the name. Some say it originated with the crew assigned to the outpost, and was intended with some degree of sarcasm. Here was a small band of men, virtually unarmed, without protection, sent to evaporate sea water in a remote location believed to be populated by armed natives. Some gift.

Salt was also made in the necks. Saltworks were located on the shores of Nassawadox Creek on Occohannock Neck. Nothing remains of the facility, but Saltworks Road still connects Jamesville with the site of the saltworks on the creek. The saltworks on Occohannock

Neck were built by Col. Edmund Scarburgh around 1660, according to Susie M. Ames, who wrote that Scarburgh also had saltworks on his property in Gargathy Neck in Accomack County.

Salt was a precious commodity and its price was fixed by the government at thirty pounds of tobacco per bushel of salt. Persons guilty of charging more, of price gouging, were fined substantial amounts to protect the public interest.

The Eastern Shore was unique in that it had a wealth of fish, and salt was readily available, so it seems likely that the two resources would have been combined to produce an important marketable commodity, salt fish. But none of the histories written about the Shore mention salt fish being used in trade with other localities, and there is little in court records that would substantiate it. Salt fish seems to have been more of a means of survival than a commodity to trade during the days of the Jamestown Colony, and this seems odd, considering that salt had been widely used to preserve food for shipping for centuries.

Salt was the ancient forerunner of refrigeration, a method of extending the useful life of foods and making it possible to ship them great distances. Mark Kurlansky, in his 2002 book *Salt – A World History*, writes that ancient civilizations learned that combining salt with other products, such as fish, increases the value of both. "More than a gastronomic development, the salting of fowl and especially of fish was an important step in the development of economies. In the ancient world, the Egyptians were leading exporters of raw foods such as wheat and lentils. Although salt was a valuable commodity for sale, it was bulky. By making a product with the salt, a value was added per pound, and unlike fresh food, salt fish, if well handled, would not spoil."

Kurlansky noted that the Egyptians did not export a great deal of salt, but they did export large quantities of salted food, especially fish, to the Middle East. "Trade in salted food would shape economies for the next four millennia," wrote Kurlansky.

Chances are, it shaped the economy of the Eastern Shore as well,

Barrel making was an important skill in the late 19th and early 20th centuries, and most communities had at least one barrel house. Barrels were used to ship potatoes, cabbages, and many other items to market via the railroad. Alton Matthews of Atlantic was the last barrel maker on the Eastern Shore. He was photographed in his shop in August 1972 and retired shortly thereafter.

but that has yet to be documented. The Shore had plentiful fish and wild game, salt was being made at several locations, and deep water landings and wharfs made shipping convenient. Salting food for shipment was likely a minor industry; it was not controlled by the James City government as was tobacco and other commodities, but was likely an artisanal product. But chances are good that shipments of goods produced locally included salt fish, canvasback ducks, and perhaps caviar made from the eggs of sturgeon, which were plentiful in local waters in those days. Even today, most rural country stores stock salted hake fish in the winter.

It has long been a tradition among local families each fall to put up filets of trout, spot, croakers, or whatever else was available in stone crocks – a layer of fish, a layer of salt – and to have salt fish during the winter when fresh fish was not available. It was always a Christmas morning tradition in our family to have salt fish and scrambled eggs for breakfast after opening the gifts. I still associate the aroma of cedar trees and the flavor of salt trout with Christmas.

The Tobacco Era

Tobacco was the first item to be traded widely and it was a major crop in the necks of the Eastern Shore. By 1632, so much tobacco was being produced in the colony that the governor issued a proclamation limiting each grower to no more than one-thousand plants. By the mid-1600s warehouses were built on local creeks and tobacco was shipped directly to Europe. Tobacco warehouses were originally built in Northampton at Kings Creek and Plantation Creek, and later at Cherrystone, Nassawadox, and Hungars. Warehouses in Accomack were on Pungoteague Creek, Guilford Creek, and Pitts Creek. The tobacco warehouse era is still reflected in place names. Warehouse Prong is a stream at the head of Pungoteague Creek, and on nearby upland is a street called Warehouse Road.

The leadership of the Jamestown Colony largely controlled the shipping of goods, with England being the primary export destination. The Eastern Shore's remote location, however, allowed local shippers more leeway in determining where products were headed. According to Susie M. Ames, the Eastern Shore enjoyed a certain independence of commerce, frequently doing business with the Dutch. Records show that tobacco was being shipped along the coast to New Netherlands and New England from the Eastern Shore, circa 1650.

The tobacco era began to wane around 1660 to 1670 for a variety of reasons, mainly because of poor markets and falling prices. But Ames believes there were two other reasons for the demise of the tobacco market: the exhaustion of the soil and the fact that there was no longer much free land available. "By the close of the century most of the area of the Eastern Shore had been patented, and the large plantations of the preceding generation were being partitioned to an increasing population," Ames wrote in *Studies of the Virginia Eastern Shore in the Seventeenth Century*.

"By 1715 there was so little interest in tobacco that Accomack petitioned the Assembly that its inhabitants might pay their public dues in pork, beef, wheat and other country commodities; but the proposition was rejected."

Historian Brooks Miles Barnes points out that another reason for the collapse of the tobacco industry on the Shore was the topography of the land. "Our creeks and inlets were too shallow for the vessels engaged in the trans-Atlantic tobacco trade," he says. "The captains of those vessels therefore ignored the Eastern Shore in favor of the deep rivers of the Western Shore. Those that did come to the Shore had to anchor at the mouths of the creeks where they took on board tobacco carried out to them in small vessels – a process both expensive and dangerous. Also, the tobacco grown on the Eastern Shore was inferior in quality to that grown in several locations on the Western Shore."

Quite a few of the early English settlers on the Eastern Shore gradually moved northward, finding that land on the northern banks of the Potomac River was amenable to growing tobacco as well as being accessible to large vessels. Many of the surnames that appeared in early Eastern Shore documents showed up later in records in Charles County and St. Mary's County, and many of those individuals held leadership positions in Maryland. Capt. William Stone, who patented land in Wilsonia Neck, was later named governor of Maryland. One of his descendants, Thomas Stone, was a signer of the Declaration of Independence. Daniel Jenifer, when his business in Gargathy Neck came to a conclusion, became a business and political leader in Maryland.

The tobacco era on the Eastern Shore was succeeded by a shift to grain and livestock. The transition was relatively seamless, according to Ames. "The comparative ease with which the transition was made may be attributed in part to the fact that it occurred before the influx of slaves into the colony during the eighteenth century, but primarily to the fact that there had been an early and continuous interest in grain and livestock and that geographical factors had fostered inter-colonial marketing. The first settlers had engaged in a diversified agriculture and, on the basis of its products, had built up a profitable trade along the Atlantic seaboard. So the decline of tobacco culture did not mean the centering of attention upon unknown commodities; it meant merely the expansion of a trade already established in other agricultural products."

Businesses and artisanal crafts on the Eastern Shore included the grinding of grain to make bread, and most necks had at least one water mill at the head of a creek. People had orchards to produce fruit, cider, and brandy, peach being a favorite. Craftsmen made bricks for construction projects using clay found near the shores of creeks. Furniture making, weaving, shoemaking, blacksmithing, and shipbuilding were all skills employed by people living in the necks. Most working wharves had facilities for building and repairing boats, and local boat builders had their own individual styles.

Long before the name Wallops became synonymous with space flight, the area was known as the home of the Wallops Neck goosery. The goosery was a farm where the Industry Down and Quilting Company of Philadelphia raised white geese, whose feathers and down would be slept upon by thousands of Americans in the 1880s.

The goosery was a boon for local grain farmers, who provided corn for the flock of geese. In 1884 the *Peninsula Enterprise* reported that the company had recently spent $1,000 among local farmers, and still was looking for more corn. "Some of our people think that if this thing continues, corn bread will be scarce," quipped a writer for the newspaper.

The goosery began operation in May 1883 when the Philadelphia corporation bought a farm in Wallops Neck from C.T. Taylor, who lived west of Wallops in Jollys Neck, which is bordered by Holden and Bullbeggar Creeks. According to the *Peninsula Enterprise*, the corporation paid $5,000 for the land, making Mr. Taylor a wealthy man. The corporation constructed quarters to house 1,900 geese on the farm.

The Planter Goes To Sea

> "Get a boat." The aunt, dreamily, as though she meant a schooner for the trade winds. "With a boat you don't need the road."
>
> Annie Proulx
>
> *The Shipping News*

The Eastern Shore's easy access to water clouded the sharp line that in other cultures divided occupations and skills. A planter might also be a mariner or a merchant, depending upon the season and the business at hand. Many planters who worked the necks of the Eastern Shore frequently had a vessel moored nearby.

Eastern Shore people are known to have an amphibious quality – equally at home on land and water. Consider my great-grandfather, John Badger, and his older brother, Thomas. Like many young men in America in 1849, they dreamed of striking it rich in the gold fields of California. Their father had died in 1846 when Thomas was 19, and he had become the leader of the family. At 15, he had taken a job as a mate on a cargo vessel, and thus began his life as a seaman.

In 1848 word spread around the world that James Marshall had discovered gold near Sutter's Fort in California. Suddenly, men by the tens of thousands took off to seek fortune and adventure in the gold fields of the west. Some traveled across country and others came by boat. Thomas and John were both experienced sailors, so they chose the latter method. They left their home port of Red Bank and sailed north to New York, and on March 3, 1849 they boarded the schooner *James L. Day* for California. They sailed from New York around Cape

This receipt is for 897 bushels of corn and 795 bushels of oats shipped to the West Indies aboard the schooner Louisiana *in 1861.*

Horn and then took a northern route up the coast. The journey took nearly six months. Thomas was 22 and John was about a month shy of 17.

Thomas remained in California for most of his life, and John eventually returned to the farm on Red Bank Creek. It is not known whether they found gold, but the experience had a profound effect on their lives. John became a planter, but he also was a mariner, and, when the opportunity presented itself, he was a merchant. John owned the schooner *Louisiana* during the years prior to the Civil War, and the *Panama* following the war. A story passed down through the family holds that Captain John got caught running a blockade during the war

This shipping manifest c. 1860 lists a cargo including turkeys, potatoes, wool, feathers, rawhide, citron, and barrels.

and forfeited the *Louisiana* to the Union navy. The *Panama* replaced it.

Family records show that John did regular business in New York and Boston, shipping produce grown on his own farm and that of others, and he seldom returned from trips to northern cities carrying ballast stones. Furniture, kitchenware, musical instruments, clothing, and tools were frequently stowed in the hold. John also did business in the West Indies, usually shipping corn, barrels of pork, pitch, tar,

Planters, Mariners, and Merchants

and lumber to the islands and returning with rum, sugar, molasses, and cocoa.

Coastal communities such as those on the Eastern Shore were unique in marrying the roles of planter and mariner. The conventional wisdom is that once a mariner patents land, clears acreage, builds a shelter, fences a pasture, and acquires livestock to care for, he in due course gives up the sea. But on the Eastern Shore, once the vast tracts patented during the early years were broken up, most farms were of a modest size – one hundred acres or so – and a landowner could spend time at sea marketing his goods as well as behind the plow during the growing season. Most small farms on the Eastern Shore had at least a few indentured servants and slaves, which made it possible for the planter to double as mariner.

Captain John was among the last to play this role. His prime years were just before and after the Civil War, and when the railroad came in the 1880s he was one of many planter-mariner-merchants on the Eastern Shore to see their careers end. It was a system that dated back to the earliest days of settlement. For mariners who settled on the Eastern Shore, the sea was never far from their thoughts, or far from their farmsteads. John had sailed around Cape Horn when he was 16; he would never be intimidated by going to sea.

Among the first of the planter-mariners was John Wallop, who patented 1,700 acres in northern Accomack County, what we know today as Wallops Neck and Wallops Island. Wallop successfully combined his career as a mariner with that of a planter, despite the vast acreage he oversaw.

According to Susie M. Ames, Robert Pitt in 1662 and 1663 patented 4,000 acres in northwest Accomack, a tract bordered by the Pocomoke River on the north, and on the west by the Chesapeake Bay and by "sunken marshes called Pitts Neck." He and his son grew crops on the land and distributed them in vessels of their own.

"The seafaring man might become a landholder and planter, but if that land had a water location, the call of the sea did not go unheeded," wrote Ames.

The planter/mariner system of the Eastern Shore had similarities in New England, where the proximity of arable land and navigable waterways on Cape Cod gave rise to sea-going farmers. Henry David Thoreau wrote in *Cape Cod*, "The inhabitants of the Cape are often at once farmers and sea-rovers...A farmer in Wellfleet, at whose house I afterward spent a night, who had raised fifty bushels of potatoes the previous year, which is a large crop for the Cape, and had extensive saltworks, pointed to his schooner, which lay in sight, in which he and his man and boy occasionally ran down the coast a-trading as far as the Capes of Virginia."

Bars and Ordinaries

Prior to the railroad days, the closest thing the Eastern Shore had to towns and villages – other than the two county seats – were the communities that often sprouted at the heads of the necks. While the necks centered on production and trade, most were linked by facilities shared in common. At the head of the neck would be a community of churches, stores, inns, bars, blacksmiths, tanneries, and perhaps an apothecary.

At the head of Church Neck is Bridgetown, a village that grew up around a bridge that spanned the headwaters of Hungars Creek, replacing a ferry that once operated there. The bridge is still in place, although today it is more of a culvert than a bridge. But if you pause for a few moments while crossing, you can see the run of the creek heading from east to west, forming Church Neck on its northern side.

Shadyside was the head of Wilsonia Neck, and at the head of Wellington Neck is the village of Franktown, which had stores, inns, and churches to serve both Black and White. The post office delivered mail to Franktown and Bridgetown, where people who lived down the neck could come to collect their correspondence. These communities, these nascent villages, were linked to each other by horse and buggy trails, one on the bayside and one on the seaside.

A common feature of the head of the neck would be the bar or ordinary, the American equivalent of the British public house. The first ordinary was licensed by Anthony Hodgskins on Old Plantation Creek and it did duty not only as a pub and inn, but as the county court as well. By the 1800s bars and ordinaries were so numerous, applications for liquor licenses were a standard part of the monthly court proceedings.

Court proceedings from October 1881 listed four new bars being licensed: to Richard P. Read at Hoffman's Wharf, James S. Nock at Assawoman, Frank P. McConnell at Chincoteague Island, and to Eli W. Bull at Bull Run (today, Daugherty). Hoffman's Wharf, now Harborton, was an appendage of Hacks Neck, Assawoman the head of Arbuckle Neck, and Bull Run the head of Custis Neck.

The court in its June 1882 session granted licenses to Louis S. Belote at Fair Oaks (Melfa), George A. Fowler at both Hawk's Nest (Mappsburg) and Sycamore Turn (probably Sycamore Bend on Finneys Creek), to Louis F. Hinman at Hunting Creek, and Revel C. Taylor at Guilford Wharf. Many of the place names were left behind when people emigrated from the necks to railroad towns in the late 19th and early 20th centuries.

Licensing bars and retail sellers was an important source of revenue for the county governments, and the court took it seriously when someone flouted the law. In the May 1883 court session, Judge Thomas C. Parramore sentenced W. S. Waterman to five days in the county jail and a fine of $18.36 for selling liquor without a license.

The court also regarded liquor and gambling as partners in crime. In July 1882, William T. Barnes and his business partners pleaded guilty to a charge of unlawful gambling at their house of entertainment at Hunting Creek, paid a fine of $115.17, and forfeited their bar room license.

The bars and ordinaries (which offered overnight accommodations) were an important part of the social fabric of the pre-railroad Eastern Shore. Saturday night at the head of the neck was a weekend celebration that ended the work week on a high note. By the time the railroad rolled in, the court was considering dozens of license applications in each session. Some of the bars would be in traditional places of business, others simply in a spare room in an applicant's home.

Many local residents made their own sprits of choice. Farms of the 19th century were diverse, and most included scuppernong grapes for making wine and peach orchards for making brandy.

Capt. John grew peaches for making brandy on his Red Bank farm. His brother Tom, who lived in California, wrote to him in January 1876 and requested a keg of peach brandy. "Ship it express from Baltimore as soon as you can," he asked, "but put the keg inside of another keg. Otherwise, someone will draw the brandy off and replace it with water."

Saturday Night at the Head of the Neck

The following account was written by Thomas G. Elliott of Accomac and was published in the August 5, 1880 issue of *Forest and Stream* magazine. It is a good example of how people who lived in the necks entertained themselves. Obviously, there was no radio, television, or internet, and in 1880 the number of people who could read for pleasure were a minority. So, the store or the ordinary at the head of the neck would be a place for the men to gather and tell stories and to perhaps have a nip of "old tangle-foot."

Perhaps the best word to describe these stories would be hyperbole, wild exaggeration. There seemed to be a competition among storytellers as to stretching the limits of imagination, and this one perhaps exceeds those limits. Storytelling was an art that thrived in ordinaries and country stores for generations on the Eastern Shore. For another good example, see Jack Melson's tale about the Yahoo of Craddock Neck at the end of the chapter on Craddock Neck.

> There was a great meeting of the "Neckers" at our store last Saturday night. After the boys had spun their yarns, in good order, some dropping quail in crossing a four-foot path, resting their arms on fence rails, killing with their guns "kicking up

Planters, Mariners, and Merchants

behind and before," bagging coons, opossums, etc., etc., Uncle Mike Jones put in an appearance by stating that his father had often related to him the prowess of his grandfather in the use of a gun, which he had imported from Holland, known as "the old pewter piece," and, amongst other things, described his wholesale destruction of blackbirds on one occasion, when he swung her around an oat stack, and killed all the way around, the charge terminating in taking off the skirts of his long-tailed blue, whereupon, being an ardent admirer of old "tangle-leg," he proposed a drink.

John Bush, whose inclinations had turned, for several years, toward the "biled owl" fraternity, having been a great listener, put in a word, which he said in no way was meant as disputing the flexibility, under curved pressure, of the gun of Mike's progenitor, stated that he, on one occasion, had made a shot somewhat alarming to tell, yet, as there still walked two living witnesses, he would relate that the occasion did not arise by putting his piece in a circular attitude, but that he held it straight from the shoulder, and left dead on the sand 350 assorted birds, curlew, snipe, etc., and, in candor, believed that as many more fluttered off, wounded, on the water.

Uncle Mike spoke up and asked: "If but one barrel?" "Only one." "What size shot?" "Fours." "Two ounce charge?" "About." "Will some gentleman be so good as to count if there are 700 pellets of fours in two ounces."

Now, you see that things began to look rather "cornerfied" for John, and as the old "tangle-foot" was working up to the usual standard, it was plain that something must be done, for the double purpose of staving off muscular action, and to drive the two heroes of the evening to an alliance, and nothing short of the "Western Farmer" could accomplish that end, so Cousin Burton stated that on one occasion a Western farmer had done wonders without good results, and he would be glad to have their attention to hear it.

Silence having been reached, this old coon hunter went on to say that this farmer had constructed a level floor for the purpose of baiting wild pigeons, and after alluring them to his place in great numbers concluded he had better secure some profits for his outlay. With a double charge in his old fusil he lashed it to two posts and lay in wait. When all things were ready, and pigeons had come in such numbers as to lead him to anticipate the need of a wagon to carry off the dead, he gave a grunt to start the birds on the wing, and pulled the cord, when lo! not one bird was left prostrated on the field, having pulled too late by one and three-quarter inches.

"Well," says Mike, "nothing very remarkable about that."

"But I was going to say that he swept up nine and half bushels of legs and feet."

"Oh! Come, John, come, s'pose we have just one nip and go."

"I don't want any," said Bush; "that pigeon affair is all that I can stand."

Sex and Violence in Gargathy Neck

Gargathy Neck does not look promising. It does not have the high banks and sandy beaches of Occohannock, nor does it have the history and architecture of Church Neck. Gargathy offers forests and farm fields, a smattering of residential units across what not long ago was a soybean field. It has a public boat launch on Gargathy Creek that provides a nice view of Metompkin Island, and, to the north, the NASA launch site on Wallops Island. Gargathy is a popular destination when NASA has an Antares launch scheduled to re-supply the space station. You can watch from the comfort of your car.

Gargathy Neck is defined by Gargathy Creek on its northern margins and Whites Creek and Mutton Hunk Branch on the south. Unlike most necks, Gargathy has no easily defined head, no community where people gathered to do business and swap the gossip of the day. The most likely candidate would be the crossroads village on Rt. 13 called Gargatha, or perhaps the Mutton Hunk community, a few homes scattered along the mysteriously named branch of the creek.

And again unlike most necks, Gargathy is not named for a family or founder or an otherwise big-wig of Eastern Shore history. In documents from 1664 the name is given as Gargaphia, which is derived from the Greek place name "Gargaphie," a secluded valley where the goddess Diana relaxed and bathed with her nymphs. And here we have our first clue that there might be more to Gargathy Neck than salt marsh and soybean stubble.

Gargathy Neck, or Gargaphia, has a history that reads like a Masterpiece Theatre classic. Change the accent from proper British to languid Eastern Shore brogue, and you will have a drama that could be a regular for months on Sunday evening public television. "It's a hoi toid on the sea soid."

Most necks are known for a specific industry or product – salt-making, agriculture, shipping, boat building. Gargathy is known for money and sex. And drama, lots of drama, and sex, illegal sex.

Three principal players star in our drama, and memorable characters they are. In order of appearance:

Edmund Scarburgh II is the product of a wealthy English family that immigrated to America around 1620. Edmund was born at St. Martin's-in-the-Fields, London, in 1617, came to America with his family, and then returned to England to have a proper education in the classics. Edmund returned around 1635, and as a young man, began accumulating thousands of acres of property on the Eastern Shore, Western Shore, and in Maryland. Along with land, Edmund acquired wealth and power, and in the mid-17th century was one of the most influential men in Virginia. He was also described as ruthless, notorious, unscrupulous, egotistical, dishonest, and one who considered himself above the law.

Mrs. Anne Toft supposedly came from England as an indentured servant when she was a small child. By the time she was 17, she had patented 800 acres on the Eastern Shore. By the time she was 21, she owned land in Gloucester County, Westmoreland County, the Eastern Shore of Maryland, and on the Caribbean island of Jamaica, a British colony. Mrs. Toft was by all accounts a woman of beauty and charm who was a cool hand when it came to negotiating a contract. She was also a woman of mystery. In legal documents of the day, she was referred to as Mrs. Toft, but there was never an appearance of a Mr. Toft, nor is there a mention of her maiden name. The title was probably part of her business plan; a married woman was generally shown respect in business negotiations. She lived at Gargaphia plantation, which was near Metompkin Road in what we now know as Gargathy Neck.

Daniel Jenifer was a handsome gentleman, recently widowed, who owned a great deal of property along the Potomac River in St. Mary's and Charles Counties in Maryland. He also speculated in land on the Eastern Shore of Virginia, and he was related to William Stone of Wilsonia Neck, who sponsored Arthur Upshur's indenture. His nephew, Thomas Stone, was the youngest signer of the Declaration of Independence. Jenifer, Scarburgh, and Mrs. Toft comprised a triangle of business and industry that has never been duplicated on the Eastern Shore. By the time the drama ends, Mrs. Toft will bear three of Edmund's children, marry Daniel Jenifer, and live with both of them, sequentially, at her plantation at Gargaphia. But it is a long story.

The Plot

The drama begins with Edmund Scarborough and Anne Toft. How they met is uncertain, but he was about 42 when they became friends, and she was 17. From all accounts, she was a beautiful, smart, ambitious, and spirited young woman, and he no doubt was attracted to her. He was a wealthy, powerful, influential man, and she was more than likely attracted to him.

But the relationship involved more than good old-fashioned lust. Anne, a teenager, had recently patented 800 acres at the head of Chesconnessex Creek and wanted more. Edmund had begun his real estate empire when he, too, was a teenager, and he likely saw something of himself in Anne – the ambition and drive, the need to excel, to own more land, to have a larger fleet of ships, to have a greater fortune than anyone else. Anne Toft to Edmund Scarburgh was perhaps a Mini-me with privileges.

This was more than a platonic friendship centered around fatherly advice. Over a period of ten years or so, Anne had three daughters, Arcadia, Atalanta, and Annabella. The father of the girls was undocumented, at least when it came to official records, but all signs pointed to Edmund. For one thing, all three children had unusual names that a man educated in the classics would be familiar with. For another, in 1664 Edmund gave Mrs. Toft a patent for a 1,200-acre tract they christened Gargaphia, a name taken from Greek mythology. They built a substantial plantation on the tract, with Scarburgh retaining lifetime rights to use the plantation for business purposes. Scarburgh had multiple industries on the property, including a saltworks, tannery, and facilities for manufacturing shoes.

Basically, Edmund bought property at Gargathy Neck, built a plantation called Gargaphia, and signed over rights to the property to Anne Toft. He regularly visited the property to manage his businesses there, and, one would assume, to enjoy the company of a younger woman who shared his passion for business and politics.

But Edmund was married, and he and his wife Mary and their children lived on the bayside on Occohannock Creek at a plantation called Hedra Cottage. Hedra was far removed from Gargaphia, which in the mid-17th century was remote and sparsely populated. Apparently, the only improvements were the Toft residence, sundry buildings dealing with the manufacture of shoes and salt, and a building called a quartering house, which was similar to an ordinary. This explains, perhaps, why Gargathy is one of the few necks that does not have a community that served as the head of the neck. The neck simply had few residents other than those at the Gargaphia compound, many of whom were transients, and a head of the neck was not needed or supported.

Despite their age difference, Edmund and Anne Toft were certainly not an odd couple, but rather had much in common. After attending school in England, Edmund arrived in Virginia in 1635 as a precocious 17-year-old. He immediately took over his father's estate and began a land acquisition program, beginning with a plantation on Magothy Bay on the seaside in Northampton County. He soon moved north and patented land on Occohannock Creek in what is now called Scarburgh Neck. He purchased a fleet of ocean-going vessels and began a shipping business, and he established a saltworks and shoe making factory on his property on Occohannock Creek.

Edmund married, built a plantation on Occohannock Creek, and he and Mary had five or six children between 1639 and 1649. By that date, Edmund owned at least 34,000 acres on both sides of the Chesapeake Bay, as well as a fleet of a dozen or more ships operating throughout the Atlantic. At the age of 31, Edmund Scarburgh was an undeniable success, but records indicate that he often pushed the boundaries of the law. "...He challenged every avenue of political and economic power, from county to courts to governors to Privy Councils, and possibly the king himself," writes John G. Kolp in *The Virginia Magazine of History and Biography*. "He captured ships, refused to pay his bills, organized his own extra-legal military units, raided Indian settlements at will, and questioned the morality of Anglican priests. In short, he did whatever he pleased whenever he pleased...."

In addition to his business interests, Edmund was very involved in the politics of the Virginia colony. He was Speaker of the House of Burgesses and at various times was High Sheriff of Accomack County, official Virginia surveyor, and an officer in the militia. He frequently was referred to as Colonel Scarburgh. In both business and politics, Edmund was a force to be reckoned with.

Anne Toft likewise began her business career at age 17, and within a decade became one of the wealthiest landowners on the Eastern Shore. According to historian Susie May Ames, Edmund amassed holdings of more than 30,000 acres over a career of thirty years, but in the 1660s alone, Anne Toft patented nearly 20,000 acres. She also operated a fleet of ocean-going ships and had various other enterprises, making her at least an equal of Edmund when it came to shrewd business dealings. A difference, however, was that Mrs. Toft knew how to keep her head down, and Edmund did not. He was very much a public figure, a blustery soul who apparently took delight in flouting laws that lesser lights were expected to adhere to. And this was the beginning of his downfall.

British laws dealing with fornication, bastardry, and adultery were very strict in the mid-17th century, and Edmund Scarburgh and Anne Toft were seemingly guilty of many of them. Fornication outside the bounds of marriage was dealt with by flogging, and a 1658 statute also demanded that both the male and female pay the parish 500 pounds of tobacco. A couple who produced a child in less than nine months of marriage could be charged, even if they had married prior to giving birth.

Edmund was a married man and had apparently been committing adultery for some ten years, and the law provided stiff penalties for this. "Adultery was a far more serious offense than simple fornication," wrote Kolp. "In the 1650s under the Commonwealth government in England, it caried the death penalty, although such extreme sentences rarely occurred."

Edmund and Anne also had three children together without being married, making their daughters bastards in the eyes of the law. "A child born out of wedlock not only indicated sinful behavior on the part of the parents, but it brought 'shame and disgrace' to the child as well," wrote Kolp. "As the 'son of nobody,' a bastard became an undesirable marriage partner and had fewer inheritance rights than those of legitimate birth....Being labeled a bastard had permanent social and legal consequences that could impact an individual's entire life."

The question, then, is how Edmund Scarburgh and Anne Toft could carry on an affair openly, producing three children, without raising the eyebrows of the courts. There were a number of reasons. As previously stated, Gargaphia was far removed from the avenues of commerce of the time. The plantation served as Anne's residence, and it was Edmund's place of business. Both were wealthy, powerful figures in the community, and Edmund and his bluster were no doubt intimidating to those who might consider bringing charges. Probably the main reason was because the Eastern Shore was very remote, separated by the Chesapeake Bay from officials at James City who might have pressed the issue. They simply did not know what was going on, or if they did, they looked the other way.

Edmund and Anne had their remote hideaway on Gargathy Neck for about six years, from the time they bought the property in 1664 to 1670, when a very public altercation shown a light on their relationship and at last brought it to the attention of officials in Jamestown.

The Toft-Scarburgh relationship began to unravel on May 8, 1670 when Edmund went to Gargaphia to oversee some of his businesses there. He was publicly confronted about his relationship with Mrs. Toft and the businesses at Gargaphia by a man named Martin Moore, who was owed money by Edmund. An altercation ensued, Edmund was seriously injured, and the case went to court two days later. Depositions from witnesses agreed that the workman had attacked the colonel, calling him "an old rogue and old dog" and vowing he "would work no more for Scarburgh's whores and bastards." The case became a permanent part of the Accomack County court records, and it doubtlessly cast a light on Scarburgh's affair that could be seen from James City.

Scarburgh had survived many previous controversies, but this one did irreparable damage to his reputation, and to that of Anne Toft. Edmund attempted a diversion by staging an "Indian attack," but the ruse did not work. In a matter of months, he was relieved of all offices and responsibilities, and within a year he had died of smallpox. He was buried near Occohannock Creek at Hedra Cottage.

"All in all, Edmund Scarburgh seems to have jousted at every windmill in his path to success, confronting fellow justices, Anglican ministers, governors, dukes, and even the king himself," wrote John Kolp. "A man with this sense of his own power and invincibility could easily have imagined that English moral codes presented no barrier to forbidden sexual relations. He may have thought he and Anne were above the law."

And now enters the third party of our entrepreneurial triangle. Daniel Jenifer and Mrs. Toft had known each other for some time. Were they lovers? No one knows for sure, but we do know that just a few weeks after Edmund's death, Anne Toft became Mrs. Daniel Jenifer. He was a man with Maryland roots, a planter and land speculator, who spent a great deal of time in Virginia and had family there. From all accounts, he was as ambitious and driven as she was. After the marriage, he moved in with Anne at Gargaphia, and the couple patented nearby land along the seaside, including Chincoteague and Assateague Islands, selling portions of it at times.

The Jenifers had a son they named Daniel of St. Thomas Jenifer (1672-1730), who received a sizeable inheritance from his parents, as did Anne's three daughters. To counter the prevailing system of primogeniture, which would favor the son or eldest daughter in estate law, the Jenifers divided a 5,000-acre section equally between the three daughters. They also left the daughters livestock, servants, and household goods, provided they did not marry before the age of seventeen without their parents' permission.

With her daughters' financial future assured, Anne appears to have backed away from the hectic business of land sales. She died in 1687 at age 45. Her three daughters married and had families of their own. Her son married and had a son also named Daniel of St. Thomas, who became a medical doctor. Like their parents, the children bought and sold land. Daniel, Jr. teamed with his half-sister Arcadia and took possession of what is now Smith Island in the Chesapeake Bay. The Jenifers were highly respected and influential people in St. Mary's County, Maryland.

The Issues

Curiously, the Toft-Scarburgh-Jenifer relationship has drawn little interest from local historians over the years. Jennings C. Wise, in his 1911 history *Ye Kingdome of Accawmacke*, mentions in an appendix that Daniel Jenifer "...married Miss Anne Toft, who was reputed to have been the wealthiest and prettiest woman then living on the Eastern Shore of Virginia." He mentions that they had a large family of children, including daughters Arcadia, Atalanta, and Arabella, but no mention is made of Edmund Scarburgh possibly being the father.

Susie May Ames makes frequent mention of Anne Toft's land holdings and wealth in her 1940 history, *Studies of The Virginia Eastern Shore in the Seventeenth Century*, but she does not mention a relationship between Toft and Scarburgh. Perhaps the historians were being deferential to prominent families and "looked the other way" when evidence might have suggested improper behavior many years ago.

Ironically, the first published mention of a possible Toft-Scarburgh relationship was made by Ralph T. Whitelaw, the architectural historian, who came across the 1670 court record showing that

Martin Moore had been sentenced to 30 lashes for attacking Edmund Scarburgh and vowing he would no longer work for his "whores and bastards." Whitelaw, of course, was researching his classic two-volume history *Virginia's Eastern Shore* when he found the records, and he mentions them somewhat extensively, writing that, "On the basis of circumstantial information, which is all that is available, the exact form of her (Toft's) relationship with Colonel Edmund Scarburgh is still an unsolved problem...."

Whitelaw also hinted that there might also be "further little-known activity" at Gargaphia, as evidenced by Anne Toft's unusually large number of tithables (taxable persons in her employ), and the presence of a "quartering house," which he described as "something less than an ordinary or tavern; perhaps an overnight guest house."

The implication is that Scarburgh and Mrs. Toft were operating a house of prostitution at their remote plantation of Gargaphia. Maryland writer Dana Kester-McCabe took that implication and ran with it in her 2020 novel, *The Persistent Buccaneer*, a work of fiction that invites the reader to speculate as to how much fact is blended into the fiction.

The closing scene on Masterpiece Theatre might be a tight closeup of the face of Martin Moore, his brow furrowed in anger as he shakes his fist at Edmund Scarburgh and swears, "I'll work no more for your whores and bastards." With those words Moore captures in an instant a relationship that for years everyone suspected, but no one confirmed.

And now, 350 years after that court session at Gargaphia Plantation, those words still accuse, but what, exactly, is the accusation? Did Edmund and Mrs. Toft produce bastard children? The jury finds them guilty. Were there whores at Gargaphia? Did Mrs. Toft import indentured girls to serve as prostitutes and thus receive patents for land? The jury is still out. The evidence, in the words of Ralph T. Whitelaw, is circumstantial.

But does it matter? Fornication happens. Get over it. The English in the 17th century were fixated with fornication and bastardry and the necessity of making the code of law adhere to the same ancient brain-shriveling dogma that gave us witch hunts and trials by fire. A child's worth and destiny could be determined by whether the mother and father had exchanged the vows prescribed by the church and the king.

My friend Miles Barnes says the enmity of the English toward bastardry had more to do with practicalities than piety. If a poor woman became pregnant out of wedlock, she and her bastard child would end up on the county dole at the taxpayers' expense. Edmund and Mrs. Toft were allowed their dalliances because they were able to support all the bastards they produced without the aid of public assistance.

Ironically, the English had no qualms about first cousins who fornicated, as long as they took the proper prefornicational vows. It was, after all, this practice that formed the foundation of rural aristocracy in Virginia. When the sons and daughters of rural aristocrats were ready to select a mate, the first event they attended was the family reunion.

Anne Toft's story is about strength and gender, a young woman who heroically ignored the constraints of gender expectation and accomplished great things. Edmund Scarburgh is both a hero and a villain, a pioneer who amassed a fortune through industry and land ownership, someone who held great power and influence, but was brought down by his total lack of humility, his certainty of entitlement. When the end came for Edmund Scarburgh, it struck with remarkable swiftness and shame. Mrs. Anne Toft Jenifer died a wealthy mother and grandmother, a woman of means who set her course in life, and followed it with determination and restraint.

When the Waterway Was Our Highway

The prevalent notion these days is that before the opening of the Chesapeake Bay Bridge in 1952 and the Chesapeake Bay Bridge-Tunnel in 1964, our peninsula was a remote, rural, wild, and somewhat backward land where people clung to old ways and pushed back against the enlightenment of modern times.

True, perhaps, but you have to realize that this thought is based upon a framework of roads, bridges, and motor vehicles. When the highway era began, water became a barrier. It isolated us. But prior to the highways and bridges, water was our means of travel, it joined us with cities north and south, it connected us with foreign countries, foreign cultures. Water was our highway; it is how we traveled and traded, how we got the food we grew and gathered to market.

It is true that the peninsula was rural, as was most of America in those days, but the Eastern Shore was no more remote than any other region. On the contrary, with our infrastructure of bays, rivers, creeks, and ocean inlets, we had a transportation system that easily connected us with each other, and with the world beyond.

Our great grand-daddies were likely more widely traveled than we are. My great-granddaddy John had a farm at Red Bank Landing and he had a sailing vessel called the *Panama* that he used to transport his crops to the market. Making trips to New York or Boston were a part of his life.

During the steamboat era, local people frequently went to Baltimore to do a little shopping. Myra Boggs of Nandua took the steamboat to Baltimore once a week to take music lessons. Folks in Baltimore often boarded a sidewheeler and took a scenic trip down the bay to Hampton, where they would spend a night or two at the hotel Hygiea, and return home relaxed and well-fed on local seafood.

In those days travel was more about the journey than the destination. Today, we have cast aside the pleasures of the journey in favor of expediency, of making the journey as brief as possible. And so we board crowded aircraft and sit elbow to elbow, our tray tables extended, a plastic cup of Coca Cola and a packet of airline pretzels in our laps, and we furtively glance at our smartphones to see how many more minutes until we are herded off, put on conveyor belts, and sent to concourse C to make our connecting flights.

Travel by steamship in the 1880s must have been the antithesis of this. Walter Lord wrote the Foreword for Alexander Crosby Brown's 1961 book *Steam Packets on the Chesapeake*, a history of the Baltimore Steam Packet Company, better known as the Old Bay Line. In it he said that steam travel combined the best virtues of north and south:

"Where the Old Bay Line got its qualities remains a mystery. Perhaps through some magical blending of the best in the North and the South, made possible by the company's unique role in 'bridging' the two regions. It is nice to think that the North has contributed its traditions of mechanical proficiency, making the ships so reliable; while the South has contributed its gracious ease, making the service so utterly delightful."

The phrase "utterly delightful" has never come to mind when making a trip up the Delmarva Peninsula, through the congestion of U.S. Route 50, across the Bay Bridge, and thence to the crowded tangle of beltways and interstates. Traveling to western Virginia would be significantly more pleasant, if not "utterly delightful," if one did not have to joust with 18-wheelers on I-64 and play a commuter version of musical chairs as traffic starts and stops in the HRB-T backup.

We live near Pungoteague Creek and it is a bit mind-boggling to realize that a century-and-a-half ago I could have gone down to Boggs Wharf, or across the creek to Evans Wharf, or to Hoffman's Wharf in what is now Harborton, and boarded a steamboat that would take me up the bay to the big city.

If I had lived on Onancock Creek I could have gone to the Hopkins Brothers steamboat office and booked passage, or to Finneys Wharf on the south side of the creek and Mears' Wharf (now Poplar Cove) on the north.

The wharves and the steamboats, of course, were a staple of neck life. That is how the farmers got their strawberries and Irish potatoes to the northern market. And that is how their wives got material and fabric from Baltimore for making draperies and clothing. Local people made frequent shopping trips to the city, often spending a few days in a boarding house or hotel while shopping or attending to other business. It was a pleasant, relaxing journey, a time to socialize with friends or to catch up on some reading while enjoying the scenery along the bay.

For children who grew up during the height of the steamboat era, it was a time they would treasure throughout their lives. E. Spencer Wise grew up in Craddock Neck but spent a week each summer with his aunt and uncle at Finneys Wharf on the south shore of Onancock Creek. The wharf was built by three Finney brothers in 1871, two years after the Eastern Shore Steamboat Company began operating their shallow-draft sidewheel steamers between Baltimore and the Chesapeake Bay tributaries on the lower Eastern Shore.

Mr. Wise was born in 1914 and graduated from Virginia Tech with a degree in agriculture. In 1992 he wrote a memoir about his boyhood days at Finneys Wharf in the 'twenties. He wrote that the wharf was busy not only during the summer during his visits, but year around, shipping everything from farm crops to oysters. "Produce harvest began with strawberries in late April or early May," he said. "Later in May came spring peas and cabbage, followed by snap beans and onions in early June. Then in late June and early July Irish potatoes, the chief crop, were harvested. Late July was a slack time, but in August the sweet potato harvest began and continued until frost. Fall snap beans and lima beans were shipped in October, and then oysters would be shipped throughout the fall and winter months."

The steamboats exported local farm and seafood products, and they brought in stock for local mercantile stores as well as fertilizer from Baltimore factories for local farmers. "There was a busy two-way traffic between Baltimore and the Eastern Shore wharfs," he wrote. "Merchants received their Christmas goods from the wholesale houses in Baltimore. Sweet potatoes that had been stored in kilns, live poultry, cedars to be used as Christmas trees, and holly were shipped to Baltimore. Barrels filled with goodies, including fresh pork from recent hog killings and dressed turkeys were shipped from the Shore to relatives and friends in Baltimore. Passengers traveled on the steamboats throughout the year."

While the Old Bay Line steamships were the "stately pleasure domes afloat" of the Chesapeake, folks who lived along the rivers and creeks of the bay were probably more familiar with smaller, more maneuverable craft that did not draw as much water. A. Hughlett Mason, a native of Harborton on Pungoteague Creek, wrote a book in 1973 titled *History of Steam Navigation to the Eastern Shore of Virginia*. Mason said that while the larger ships of the Old Bay Line were vital to commerce on the bay, the rural areas depended upon smaller, shallow-draft vessels. "Even though everyone planned with enthusiasm a trip to Baltimore or Norfolk, the economy of the area was largely based on the excellence of transportation facilities for all kinds of commodities to and from Baltimore," Mason wrote.

Steam-propelled boats first appeared on the bay in 1813, and in 1838 steamboat service became available on Virginia's Eastern Shore when the *Virginia* stopped at what is now Harborton on her regular runs between Baltimore and Norfolk. This was a watershed event for transportation in the rural area. The era of commercial public transport had begun. You no longer had to own a boat and possess navigational skills to travel the bay. You could buy a ticket, board at the wharf of your choice, and relax with the *Baltimore Sun* as the steamer headed north to the city. You could even book a stateroom and get a good night of rest while you travelled. The railroad would not open for nearly a half-century, so steamships provided local people a comfortable and comparatively rapid connection with the outside world.

"This section was inestimably more fortunate than the great landlocked areas of Virginia, which were forced to depend on stage coaches and wagons for transportation until the advent of the railroads," wrote Mason.

Steamboat service on the Eastern Shore was interrupted by the Civil War, but it resumed with vigor in 1867 when the Eastern Shore Steamboat Company was organized. The company was founded by the Harlan and Hollingsworth boat building firm of Wilmington, Delaware, which soon had a network of steamers operating from Baltimore to the Pocomoke River and down the bayside of the Eastern Shore to Northampton County. Most creeks, depending upon depth, would have steamboat landings on both the north and south shores, serving clients from two necks.

The golden years for Eastern Shore necks were the two decades separating the end of the Civil War and the opening of the railroad in the 1880s. The steamboat era blended with the era of sail to make the Eastern Shore something of a legend when it comes to commerce by water. Independent operators were important to local planters and shippers, but the Eastern Shore Steamboat Company provided dependable, scheduled service between northern markets and rural wharves that served the necks. The era of public transportation brought great changes to the lives of Eastern Shore residents.

Myra Boggs came from a family of mariners who operated an independent shipping business out of Nandua. In July 1956 she discussed the steamboat era with the *Peninsula Enterprise* newspaper of Accomac. At that time, the day of the steamboats was near its end, and Mrs. Boggs reminisced about an era that she called "beyond description."

Her father and his five brothers operated a bay and coastal freight trade using sailing craft. Their uncle was one of the best known pilots on the coast, and the family was widely known for coastal and ocean commerce. "I was born and am still living at Nandua,...and with this background and having always lived near the water, naturally, I inherited a love for watercraft and their times," she said.

The necks of the bayside were served principally by three sidewheel steamboats: The *Sue*, the *Helen*, and the *Eastern Shore*. All were built by Harlan and Hollingsworth in the two decades following the Civil War, and each vessel was finely finished and its crew noted for friendly service." My mother, then a young lady, lived on the north shore of Pungoteague Creek, a little west of the present Harborton, and I've heard her tell of the *Sue*, ... a seemingly floating palace, and of the excitement whenever the steamboat arrived at different landings," said Mrs. Boggs.

Evans Wharf and Boggs Wharf were other landings on Pungoteague Creek. Evans was on the north side of the creek and served farmers and residents in the Cashville and Mt. Nebo area. Boggs Wharf was across the creek from Evans Wharf and provided service to Yeo Neck residents. Both landings are well up the creek and the water is shallow, making navigation a challenge even for experienced captains and the shallow-draft vessels they ran. "The water was not deep near Boggs Wharf," said Mrs. Boggs. "The officials said a steamboat could not land there. My uncle, Captain Frank Boggs, insisted it could. He persuaded them to let him try it. He took over the wheel, brought the craft up the stream, turned the steamboat around and made the landing without a hitch."

Mrs. Boggs grew up during the height of the steamboat era in an area that depended upon boats for both travel and commerce. "The wharf at Nandua was a part of our home property -- and only several hundred yards from the house. In my childhood the shore line was of beautiful hard sand. Between the water's edge and the road to the wharf was a wide stretch of white sand. This is now grown up in grass and the shore is muddy. In former years the children of Nandua gathered here and built villages of sand houses, some of them with hallways big enough to crawl through. When the steamboat came to the wharf all the children would go to the shore and jump the waves."

The principal cargo of the steamboats consisted of agricultural products. White potatoes, called Irish potatoes, were the early summer crop, and sweet potatoes were shipped in the late summer. "Nandua was more than a playground for children," said Mrs. Boggs. "It was one of the biggest shipping points on the Eastern Shore of Virginia. I've known as many as two boats to load here in a day -- and still leave vehicles (carts, wagons and a few trucks) in line for a quarter mile out the road waiting to be unloaded."

Mrs. Boggs said numerous boats served the bayside creeks over the years, but the most popular was the *Eastern Shore*. "The best loved of all was the grand old side-wheeler, the *Eastern Shore*. It was on the *Eastern Shore*, while studying music in Baltimore, I made seventeen trips in seventeen weeks."

Today, it is difficult to envision steamships navigating the winding, shallow creeks of the bayside. Of course, the water was much deeper in 1870 than it is today. Many years of farming waterfront land has caused runoff and siltation that has transformed once navigable waterways into tidal flats. But these were large boats to be maneuvering in bayside creeks even then, and many waterways were too shallow to accommodate the passenger steamers.

The first Eastern Shore Steamboat Company steamer to be used on the Shore, the *Sue*, measured 175 feet in length and drew ten feet of water. She came to the Shore in 1867 when she was new from the factory in Wilmington, and she ushered in the era of passenger steamers

Steamer, Eastern Shore

in fine style. "A palace afloat," was a frequently used description. When new, the *Sue* operated to Crisfield and Pungoteague, Hungars, and Cherrystone Creeks. Later she was used on the York, James, and Potomac Rivers. She was retired from service in 1924.

The *Sue* was replaced on the Shore in 1871 by the *Helen*, which was smaller and more maneuverable in narrow, shallow creeks. The *Helen* was 150 feet in length and drew seven feet of water. Both the *Sue* and the *Helen* were under the command of George A. Raynor.

The crown jewel of the Eastern Shore Steamboat Company was the *Eastern Shore*, which began service in April 1883. She was a beloved passenger steamer, but her chief purpose was to transport farm produce. According to A. Hughlett Mason's *History of Steam Navigation to the Eastern Shore of Virginia*, her freight deck extended eleven feet over her hull, and she could pack 3,500 bushels of Irish potatoes. The *Eastern Shore* was 176 feet in length and had a depth of 9.5 feet. She sailed for 55 years out of Baltimore and transported about 300 passengers per week. George Raynor also captained this vessel for a long period of time.

To get an idea of the relative size of these vessels, the old ferry steamers that until 1964 sailed between Kiptopeke and Little Creek were about 250 feet long and had a depth of about 20 feet. The *Delmarva*, built in 1933, had a length of 339 feet. She served as the Kiptopeke ferry and later, when the bridge-tunnel opened, was transferred to the Lewes-Cape May route. Her name was changed to the *Cape May*.

The Eastern Shore Steamship Company ended passenger service in 1932 and thus an era ended. It was remembered by many not so much as a means of travel, but an opportunity to gather with friends and renew acquaintances. This was especially true for people who lived in the necks and made use of the steamboats on a regular basis. Myra Boggs of Nandua knew the crew members well and thought of them as friends.

"During the time of the Eastern Shore Steamboat Company Mr. T. A. Joynes was the purser on the Eastern Shore," said Mrs. Boggs. "He was a most agreeable host to travelers, as was Frank Battaile and many acting as pursers, as well as the different captains and various others, including Mr. Foster, the night watchman, and Ned Brittingham, who left steamboating to go back to the Alaskan Yukon in search of gold. Everyone on the boat, deck hands and waiters, were faithful to their trust and did all in their power to add to passenger comfort and pleasure. Not the least of these was Jonah Bradford, a colored man, who for many years was head waiter."

"If the boat was not too crowded some of us would dance, or perhaps gather around the piano and have an informal song fest," she said. "Yes, for the most part, it was like a big family party on a pleasant outing. The food was excellent, well served, everything in abundance and price for dinner was 50 cents. The boats were kept spotlessly clean. Many Baltimoreans made the round trip just for pleasure."

Margaret Twyford's Occohannock Neck

Margaret Malana Twyford was the valedictorian of the 1934 graduating class at Franktown-Nassawadox High School, and she was chosen to write the McMaster Old Home Essay and read it at the graduation ceremony. The McMaster essay was established in 1909 to encourage students to write about the history of the area where they lived. The writer received the McMaster medal at graduation.

Margaret and her parents, Mr. and Mrs. Roland Twyford, lived in Wardtown, the head of Occohannock Neck, so Margaret decided to write about her home neck. Wardtown had numerous houses, nine stores, a mill, a church, and a steamboat wharf down the road at Read's (now Morley's) Wharf. It was a wonderful farming area, bordered on the north by Occohannock Creek, on the west by Chesapeake Bay, and on the south by Nassawadox Creek.

The McMaster Essay program was a great idea. It encouraged students to learn about local history, and it produced a wealth of documents that captured local history in a naïve, matter-of-fact fashion. High schools all over Delmarva participated, and the Nabb Center at Salisbury University today has a collection of eight boxes of essays, covering four linear feet, dating from 1932 to 2015. The Eastern Shore of Virginia Heritage Center at the public library in Parksley has a collection of essays produced by schools in Accomack and Northampton.

The Old Home essays tend to be a blend of fact and folklore, and the idea was brilliant in that it encouraged bright young people to interact with older neighbors, and get oral history into print. "Tell me about your days on the ferry boats, Grandpa."

Margaret began with the Native Americans, writing that "The first white settler that there is any record of in Occohannock Neck was Thomas Johnson. Sir William Berkeley, Governor of Virginia, granted 1,000 acres of land to him in 1647. In 1650 Ochiawampe, an Indian chief known as the King of the Eastern Shore, sold part of Occohannock Neck to Edmund Scarburgh. Ochiawampe wrote the deed on a stump in the Mill Branch about one-third mile from Wardtown. Now the deed is on record at Eastville. Ochiawampe, when he died in 1656, left in his will that his tribe should live either at Wachapreague or in Occohannock Neck. If they chose Wachapreague the whites could use Occohannock Neck as they pleased."

Margaret's narrative, written in 1934, was remarkably accurate. Ralph T. Whitelaw, in his 1951 classic, *Virginia's Eastern Shore*, confirmed that Johnson was the first owner, and the acreage given by Whitelaw differs only slightly from Margaret's. The agreement among the natives reflects oral history handed down from generation to generation like a favorite family recipe.

The church was a vital part of life at the head of the neck, and Wardtown and Jamesville had several churches of different faiths over the years. In the rural necks of the Eastern Shore, the church not only dealt with the spiritual needs of a congregation, but also contributed to the social and economic well-being of the community. Church socials, community dinners, and holiday celebrations brought the church family together on a regular basis. In the days before welfare and social services, the church gave its attention to the needy or to those who had suffered some sort of misfortune.

"The first church at Jamesville was a Methodist Church and was called Bethel." wrote Margaret. "The oldest inhabitants do not remember when this church was started and we have no record of it. It was low and small and at one end there was a gallery where the slaves sat. Some of the early preachers were Rev. Wesley Elliott, Rev. Haldrup, Rev. Herbert, and Rev. Humphrey. This church was too small so it was moved off and used for a schoolhouse. Later, it was sold to William Thomas Ashby who moved it to his farm and turned it into a dwelling, and it is used for a dwelling today."

The Bethel Church that stands today was built on the original site in 1883, and is the only church in the neck. A Northern Methodist Church was built near Bethel around 1890, and this church was done away with about 1900, according to Margaret. "A Baptist church was built near Wardtown in 1896, and this church was disbanded in 1917."

Industries in Occohannock

The fertile soils of Occohannock Neck have made it one of the principal agricultural areas of the Eastern Shore, and farming was central to the import and export economy of the region. But according to Margaret, the first industry in the neck was salt-making. "Salt was made at a place on Nassawadox Creek, and due to the fact that salt was made there, the place is called Saltworks today."

Salt was made on the barrier islands to support the Jamestown Colony by providing a method of preserving fish and other protein for use during the winter when food was scarce, but salt also was made at several locations on the mainland Eastern Shore. Col. Edmund Scarburgh made salt on his property near Craddockville on the bayside and in Gargathy Neck on the seaside. Salt was distilled from seawater by an evaporation process, and the price of the valuable commodity was controlled by the colonial government to avoid price-gouging by salt dealers. Old maps show a saltworks on the south end of Assateague Island. The saltworks have been gone for centuries, but Saltworks Road still links the community of Jamesville with the site where salt was distilled on the banks of Nassawadox Creek.

Cottage industries of various types began in the necks of the Eastern Shore, and Occohannock had its share. "John Addison made molasses and brown sugar at Mount Airy, an old place near Concord Wharf," according to

Margaret. "He grew all of the sugar cane that he used to make the products."

Mills were an important part of the communities in the necks, and they played a variety of roles. Mills were used to produce lumber for construction projects such as homes, barns, and boats, and mills were used to grind grain such as corn and oats to make bread.

"The first sawmill was at Wardtown before the Civil War," Margaret wrote. "This sawmill was owned by Wales Ward. The next sawmill was at Saltworks right after the Civil War. This one was owned by a Mr. Wilson. Later one was at Concord Wharf and it was owned by a Mr. Hastings. This mill blew up and blew a man into the water."

Grain was ground in mills powered by the tidal flow of creeks and also those powered by wind. "At Sheep's Branch there used to be a watermill," according to Margaret. "When there wasn't enough water to run a mill, there were windmills to grind the corn and wheat. There was a windmill at Battle Point. The watermills stayed around here a longer time than the windmills. When the watermills were discarded, corn was ground at the sawmills."

Residents of the necks needed items such as coffee and sugar and other commodities they could not grow on their farms or gather from nearby bays, so stores appeared in communities near wharves where ships would land with wares from distant cities. "Joshua Stewart was one of the first storekeepers in the Neck," according to Margaret. "He kept a store on Nassawadox Creek near Saltworks around 1859. Another store was built on Nassawadox Creek in 1865 by A.N.H. Mapp. The next stores were at Jamesville and at the steamboat wharves. The Neck has built up until at present (1934) there are nine white stores."

Margaret wrote that most of the people who lived in the neck went to Belle Haven to get their mail. Belle Haven was on the bayside stagecoach route linking Drummondtown with Pungoteague, Hadlock, Franktown, Bridgetown, Johnsontown, Shadyside, and Eastville. "The first post office opened at Jamesville around 1882," according to Margaret. "H.P. James, Jr. was the first postmaster and he opened the first mail bag. At one time Hamp, a negro, carried the mail from Exmore to Jamesville on his back. Later, he rode horseback and carried the mail, and still later, he carried it in a road cart."

Occohannock Neck was virtually surrounded by water, and seafood supplemented an economy that depended heavily on agriculture. "Captain Scott and A.N.H. Mapp planted the first oysters in Nassawadox Creek in 1865" wrote Margaret. "Tank Ames shipped a barrel of oysters on the *Helen* in 1881 and it took only 85 oysters to make the barrel. The chief crops in the early days were corn, tobacco, wheat, and cotton. Now the chief crop is potatoes."

The Steamboats and the Wharfs

Then, and now, the major industry in Occohannock Neck was agriculture. Farm crops needed to get to market, and the neck had several wharfs to serve that purpose. Read's Wharf, now Morley's, is a short distance north of Wardtown on Occohannock Creek, as is Concord Wharf. In the southern part of the neck, James Wharf and the Saltworks Wharf were on Nassawadox Creek.

Years ago, Read's Wharf was not simply a point of embarkation, but a destination all its own. George H. Read, a northerner, bought a 200-acre farm on the south shore of Occohannock Creek after the Civil War and built vacation houses, a fishing pier, a store, bar, and post office, and began entertaining guests, many of whom came for hunting and fishing. So, when the steamers from Baltimore arrived, it was not uncommon for a few passengers to linger for a few days.

The business thrived in the 1880s and a community grew up around the wharf. Groundbreaking for Melson Methodist Church was held in September 1889, with an all-day fair and festival planned to celebrate the occasion, and private residences were built in the neighborhood. Thomas Johnson, from Wilmington, Delaware, built a steam sawmill at his home, Highland Light, in 1889.

A report in the Hartford, Connecticut *Telegram* in 1890 gave a glowing account of a visit by two New England men who said that thousands of pounds of fish were being shipped to Baltimore and Philadelphia markets each week from Read's Wharf. In addition, there were "oyster beds running for a mile along the shore, soft shell crabs lying there ready to be caught, every kind of vegetable possible...in addition to which he (Read) raises, fattens and kills all his own beef, mutton, poultry, rabbits, tame geese, and wild geese...and game is abundant all about his house."

Unfortunately, Read's resort lasted only a few years. The large store on the property was burned in 1890 by burglars who were trying to destroy evidence of their crime. George Read died in 1892 and his widow, Betty, put the property up for sale. The property was taken over by the Eastern Shore Steamboat Company, and later became the property of the Morley family. At that time, it was known mainly as a shipping point as the era of steamships flourished on the Eastern Shore.

"The first steamboat to come into Occohannock Creek was named *Sue*," according to Margaret. "This boat landed at Concord Wharf about 1867. The captain was Captain George A. Raynor. Due to the fact that she drew so much water, this boat couldn't be used in Occohannock Creek."

Margaret said that the *Helen*, a shallow-draft vessel, was used in Occohannock Creek. "The steamboat company tried to establish a line in Nassawadox Creek, but after making the first trip they found that there wasn't enough water. The smaller *Helen* made the trip to Nassawadox around 1872 and landed at Saltworks Wharf. Captain George A. Raynor was captain and Captain Jim Arnold piloted the boat in."

The glory days of the steamboat era came in the mid-1880s, just before the railroad transformed shipping on the Eastern Shore. The signature vessel of the steam era was aptly named the *Eastern Shore*. The boat made her first trip in May 1883. "The *Eastern Shore* was considered a floating palace at that time," wrote Margaret. "Captain George A. Raynor brought her out on her trial trip and he remained captain of this boat until a short while before he died."

All three of the boats that served Occohannock Neck – the *Sue*, *Helen*, and the *Eastern Shore* – were owned by the Eastern Shore Steamboat Company, according to Margaret. "Tully Joynes from Onancock started with this company and stayed with it util he was pensioned a few years before he died. He was the last living member of the company. From time to time, different steamboats have come into Occohannock Creek but the *Helen* in the only one that went into Nassawadox Creek."

Fun Times

Occohannock was not all about agriculture, industry, and shipping. The sandy beaches and Chesapeake Bay frontage made the neck a vacation destination for Eastern Shore residents and for people from northern cities as well. Battle Point was once a well-known vacation spot, and Silver Beach for generations has been a summer community. In the years before air conditioning became prevalent in modern homes, many local families retreated to a beach cabin to spend at least a few weeks during the summer.

According to Margaret, the tradition of gathering at Silver Beach began after a church service on a sweltering Sunday when several of the parishioners decided that a perfect benediction would be a lengthy soak in the salty waters of the Chesapeake Bay at what became known as Silver Beach. "One hot Sunday morning at church a few people decided they would go down to Silver Beach," she wrote. "The men went in swimming. This incident grew into general practice, and from that time it has been quite a popular gathering place for the people of the Eastern Shore."

Silver Beach has been a popular gathering place for generations of Eastern Shore residents. Families vacationed there, and folks would visit Lil's, a popular gathering spot, for a game of pool or conversation with friends. Battle Point, however, was a gathering place long before Silver Beach and Lil's came along. The name reflects a Revolutionary War battle fought in Occohannock Neck.

"One of the battles on the Eastern Shore was fought in the neck, wrote Margaret, "and today we call the place Battle Point. The American army was led by Col. Christian. I have not been able to find out the leader of the British army. It has been told to me that the Americans won."

According to Margaret, Battle Point became one of the leading summer resorts on the bayside, and its popularity extended beyond Occohannock Neck. People came for the sandy beach, but it was the weekend boat races that drew the crowds. The resort was owned originally by a northern man named Booth, who opened the resort shortly after the end of the Civil War.

"He built a large pier, a hotel, and places for amusement," according to Margaret. "People came in boats from far and near to watch the boat racing. There were two towers from which the women watched the racing. One of the outstanding boat races was between a canoe called *Dolly Varden* and the skiff called *Janie*. The *Dolly Varden* won, and the race was for a long time known as the *Dolly Varden* Race. The skiff *Janie* is now in Upshur's boathouse at Brownsville. Some other places of amusement were ten-pin alleys and places for women to play croquet."

Margaret indicated that in the later years a man named Benners bought Battle Point and built a large wharf there for shipping lumber. The site of the resort and the boat houses are now out in the bay.

Schools

Margaret Twyford's history of Occohannock Neck came exactly fifty years after the NYP&N Railroad opened for business on the Eastern Shore. Her essay is a testimony to the vast changes brought by the railroad, especially in rural areas such as the necks, where the focus quickly changed from inward issues of daily survival to more progressive concepts such as education and the realization that the ability to read and write is as fundamental to survival today as was the ability to handle a boat or to coax a crop of corn from the ground fifty years ago.

The railroad meant days were numbered for Saturday nights at the head of the neck, male-dominated testosterone fests in which oral traditions steeped in "old tangle-foot" provided bleary-eyed entertainment and lubricated the passage of time. The railroad was followed in short order by the motor car, improved roads, and railroad towns such as Exmore, Parksley, and Cape Charles where residents enjoyed electric lights, indoor plumbing, and department stores such as Benjamins in Exmore, which offered fashions and housewares once found only in the cities. The head of the neck had gone from the heart of a community to an archaic institution victimized by a bloodless coup d'état that left it limp and in ruins.

The steamships still sailed from the necks, but the focus of business and the pulse of the Shore's economy emphatically shifted to the railroad towns. Ironically, a century later, the focus would shift once more, when, sparked by increasing traffic on the Chesapeake Bay Bridge-Tunnel, U.S. Route 13 would be widened and re-routed, leaving railroad towns like Onley, Cape Charles, Exmore, and Parksley as crippled and hollow as were the heads of the necks during the revolution of 1884.

The opening of the railroad broadened the horizons of the Eastern Shore, and with this came an awakening of the need for education. The ability to read and write was considered a fundamental need that must be met by the community; it was no longer a luxury available only to those who could afford it. At the beginning of the 20th century, more than one-quarter of the people who lived in Accomack and Northampton Counties could not read or write. By the year 1920, the total still hovered around 20 percent, according to census figures.

Education came slowly to the necks, but, gradually, those comfortably insulated from the wider world began to peel away the layers and realize what awaited them. Perhaps it was the influence of railroad

Franktown High School in Nassawadox

itself, bringing goods from distant places, visitors who came from northern cities wearing the aura of wealth and knowledge. Perhaps it was the newspapers that came each day bringing news of the world, for those able to able to decipher it. Perhaps it was the popular periodicals of the time, the colorful magazines that promised happiness to the willing consumer. Or it could have been war, the Great War and the seduction of patriotism, a nationalistic fervor that awakened a call to arms, a conviction to take up the battle of the righteous, a feeling again of the kinship of a united people who had been torn asunder generations ago by the wreckage of secession.

The rural church was a leader in social change during the 19th century. Before the days of government-funded public welfare, the church heeded its scriptural call to heal thy brother. In the years prior to the Civil War the church helped to educate the children.

Margaret wrote that there was a school at Wardtown in 1858 that on Sundays doubled as a Sunday School. "The land for this school was given by Mr. and Mrs. Cornelius Ward. Whether this was a public school or not I do not know. In 1859 a public school was started at Jamesville. The state gave $300 a year for this school. It was taught by Abel Thomas Ashby, who at that time was a young man out of college. He didn't think $300 a year was enough for his teaching, so after Christmas holidays six patrons agreed to give $50 each if he would stay and teach. Those patrons were Jimmie Ashby, Ben Ashby, Hez James, John Colonna, Long Smith, and John Stewart. Later this schoolhouse was moved away and school was taught in the old church by Ed Mapp."

The early attempts at education on the Shore generally focused on well-to-do families. Tutors were available to teach the basics to the children of wealthy planters, and the offspring of the very wealthy were frequently sent to boarding schools, often back in England.

The Virginia General Assembly in 1845 passed legislation allowing communities to form school districts and to levy taxes for free schools, and villages in both counties participated. By 1850 Accomack had 27 one-room schools with an enrollment of 1260 pupils. Northampton had 13 such schools with 622 pupils. The schools were open free of charge to children between the ages of six and 21 living in the district.

The modern era of the public school system began in October 1870 when the state commissioned school superintendents for both counties. Graded schools were added, and many schools had more than one teacher. By 1885 Accomack had 82 public schools and Northampton had 26. In addition, there were numerous private schools and tutors available to educate many children.

"In 1887 a school was built in the lower neck," wrote Margaret. "Around the same time a school was built in Jamesville. Later, Wardtown and Jamesville schools consolidated, and when that happened a school was built where the Wardtown school stands today. Its course included the first nine grades."

Consolidation of schools had its advantages and drawbacks. Consolidation added variety and depth to the academic offerings, as well as opportunities for students to participate in extracurricular activities such as sports, drama, and music. The drawback, especially for families living in the rural necks, was that schools were often some distance from the students' homes; the era of the community school had ended.

When the Franktown and Nassawadox schools consolidated around 1912-13, students from the farms and villages in the neck had to provide their own way of getting back and forth to school. A testimony to the value people placed on education is reflected in the number of graduates who had to navigate muddy roads to get to school. "In the graduating class of 1916 there were four students from Wardtown," according to Margaret. "Namely, they were Joseph Ennis, Milton Heath, Vernon Richards, and Burleigh Turner. Since then, there have been 56 graduates from Franktown-Nassawadox, which makes a total of 60 representing Occohannock Neck. Before 1920 these pupils provided their own way to and from school, some driving twenty or more miles daily."

The first school bus came to Occohannock Neck in 1920, but it was not exactly chauffeured transportation. "School officials agreed to provide a Ford school bus to transport the students, but the terms were that a pupil had to volunteer to drive the bus without pay," Margaret wrote. "Thomas Ashby drove this bus for two years and Samuel Ashby and Harry Mapp for one year each, carrying the responsibility in a commendable manner. Then Horace Wilkins was employed as a regular truck driver for ten years, establishing a very fine record in the service."

When the new Exmore-Willis Wharf High School opened in the fall of 1926, a bus was provided to transport students from the neck to that school. "Since then, two buses have been used to transport the pupils of the neck to Franktown-Nassawadox and Exmore-Willis Wharf. The Jamesville school was closed in 1930 and the Wardtown school in 1932, but the buildings and land are still owned by the Northampton County School Board," wrote Margaret.

Education in Occohannock Neck supports the theory that the more difficult it is to accomplish something, the more highly it is valued. Students who graduated from the neck schools, and later the consolidated schools, had to earn their educations. They had to rise early, return home late, and handle the chores of farm life before and after the sun made its appearance. Not surprisingly, many of the students did not end their education at Franktown-Nassawadox. "Fifty percent of the Franktown-Nassawadox graduates from the neck have gone further with their education in college and university, and they are now distributed in sixteen different professions," Margaret wrote with obvious pride.

"The most urgent need of Occohannock Neck at present is the completion of the hard-surfaced road," she wrote. "This improvement will greatly facilitate the economic life and add to the comfort of all children in their educational life."

Sometimes the Quiet Ones Tell the Best Stories

Craddock is one of those quiet, unassuming necks that has not produced political leaders such as the Upshurs of Church Neck. It lacks deep-water creeks that might have fostered early economic growth. And it does not have the scenic, high bluffs of Occohannock or the towering dunes of Savage Neck. Craddock Neck has avoided the entrepreneurial lust of land developers and has no cookie-cutter communities with streets named for ducks.

Craddock Neck has produced generations of solid Eastern Shore families, good people who have farmed the land, started businesses, built churches and schools, and in many other ways have made the Eastern Shore a better place to live. Oh, and Craddock Neck is home to a mythological creature called the Yahoo, a curious being that on certain nights rises out of the swamp and makes an eerie sound that for generations has sent shivers down the spine of those who hear it. The creature was first encountered in the late 1700s and it still is around today, sometimes heard, but never seen. We will have more on it after a bit of background.

Although I have never lived in Craddock Neck, I do have some personal involvement in the place. Years ago, I worked in the newspaper business with Bill Sterling, who had just graduated from the University of Richmond and was hired by George McMath, owner of *The Eastern Shore News*, to cover sports for the paper. Bill and I worked together for some ten years and have been friends for more than forty. When we weren't in the newsroom in Accomac, we were likely either in a duck blind or in a boat fishing for trout off Onancock Creek, depending upon the season.

Bill's heritage runs deep through Craddock Neck. He grew up in Craddockville, the head of the neck, and many generations of his family farmed land that drained into either Craddock or Nandua Creek. Bill said the farm was purchased in the 1800s by his great-great-grandfather for $800.

Bill used to talk about putting out seed sweet potato sprouts when he was a kid. One day, while putting out potato sprigs under the hot sun, Bill decided he would prefer to write about sports for a living. He built a house on Craddock Creek where he keeps his Carolina Skiff at the ready.

Another long-time Craddock Neck friend is Jackie Farlow. Jackie grew up in Craddock's historic home, called Craddock, or Currituck, which her family bought in 1900. Her father, Captain Jack Melson, was a farmer and waterman in the neck.

Jackie married Charlie Farlow of Quinby, a career coast guardsman, and when Charlie retired he went to work for The Nature Conservancy, fittingly as keeper of the Machipongo Inlet Coast Guard Station on Hog Island, which TNC had purchased. During the late 1970s and early 1980s, TNC assembled the Virginia Coast Reserve, a sanctuary of some 30,000 acres of barrier islands and seaside farms and marshes.

Charlie and Jackie teamed up to manage the old station. He took care of the physical needs of the building, which had become run down since being deactivated by the coast guard, and Jackie cooked meals for the dozens of volunteers who came to the island to clean, paint, cut brush, haul away trash, or any other of the endless tasks that needed to be done to bring the station back to life. When renovated, the station was used for years to temporarily house researchers and to give potential donors a close-up look at the landscape TNC was working to protect. Unfortunately, the building was destroyed by fire after being struck by lightning.

The Conservancy had no trouble enlisting volunteers because they were lured to the island by Jackie's cooking, which became legendary. There would be fresh fish taken from local waters, clams and oysters, and perhaps black duck and dumplings during hunting season. My wife, Lynn, worked for TNC and our family were regular guests at the station. Hog Island was a part of our son's upbringing (Charlie once changed his diaper.), and I think we have Hog Island, the Nature Conservancy, and the Farlows to thank for giving Tom a lifetime interest in nature. There were no video games on Hog Island; clamming and birdwatching were the usual past-times.

The home Jackie grew up in, Craddock, was built around 1798. The original home on the site was destroyed by fire in 1778, reportedly by British soldiers, and had once been the home of Rev. Thomas Teackle, an Anglican minister who served for forty years on the Eastern Shore. He was the original rector of what is now St. George's Church in Pungoteague. Rev. Teackle played a prominent role in the story of the Yahoo of Craddock Neck, and we will hear more from him shortly.

My dentist when I was a young man was Dr. William H. Turner, who, if you haven't guessed by now, was a product of Craddock Neck, and one of its more colorful and controversial products as well. Dr. Turner, and his son David, are two of the most prominent wildlife sculptors in America today. But before Dr. Turner gained fame as a sculptor, he needed to find a way to support his family. The answer was dental school, and Dr. Turner opened a practice in the town of Accomac and operated it until he could pay the bills by selling sculptures of birds and animals.

Around the time the sculpting business began to prosper, Dr. Turner's eldest son, Bill, also graduated from dental school, and he immediately took over his dad's practice in Accomac. Story has it that Dr. Turner was in the process of replacing a filling in a patient's molar when he casually handed over the tray of dental instruments to Bill, removed his white jacket, and calmly walked out of the building.

If that story involved anyone other than Dr. Turner, I would be disinclined to believe it. But having gotten to know him pretty well, I have no doubt it is true. He is one of Craddock Neck's most brilliant, colorful, exasperating sons, frequently a thorn in the side of local government, a talented artist and writer whose stories about growing up in Craddock Neck are wonderful.

The Landscape

You reach Craddock Neck from the north by taking Route 178 south from Pungoteague. At Craddockville, Rt. 178 makes a sharp left turn and heads southeast toward Shields, Belle Haven, Hadlock, Franktown, and other points south. This is the old bayside road that connected pre-railroad communities from northern Accomack to Cherrystone in Northampton County. Ignore the left turn and continue past the church into downtown Craddockville, turn right onto Rt. 614 and you will be on Craddock Neck Road. This is rural country, forests and farm fields, with homes scattered here and there, but no concentrated housing developments. Craddock Neck Road ends at the confluence of several private farm lanes. A branch, Teackle Road, ends a short distance farther in the driveway of the old Teackle home.

The neck is formed by Craddock Creek on the southern margin, and Currituck and Nandua Creeks on the north. Beyond the end of the road is a massive wetland called Hyslop Marsh, which faces the Chesapeake Bay. Local residents recall a landing where steamboats would dock called Martin's Wharf, but its location is a mystery and the waters surrounding Craddock Neck are very shallow. It could be that Martin's Wharf was associated with the old Teackle Farm, but there is no listing in Whitelaw of a Martin owning property in Craddock Neck. It is more likely that Martin's Wharf was north of Craddock Neck on Hacks Neck, where the Martins were prominent owners of property and businesses.

On old maps, Craddockville is referred to as Turkey Pens. Where the pens were located, and who owned them, is a mystery. The name lives on though in the form of the Turkey Pen Pickers, a loosely associated group of musicians who get together now and then for jam sessions at the Chair Place, a former general store where Bill Aeschliman opened a chair repair shop. The big front room is an eclectic mix of wooden chairs in various states of repair, musical instruments hanging from the walls, and assorted amplifiers, microphones, and speakers, all linked by a grapevine of tangled wires. In an earlier life, the old building that houses the Chair Place was one of many businesses in Craddockville that served the farming families of the neck and surrounding countryside.

On an afternoon in early 2023, a group of current and former Craddock Neck residents got together at the home of Anne Sterling to talk about growing up in the neck. Anne was looking forward to celebrating her ninety-first birthday, and with her were her close friends Trissie Colonna, Nancy Byrd Camden, Jo Sue Drummond Parker, and Jimmy Smith, who has spent most of his life in the neck. Over cookies and iced tea, old friends brought out photographs and talked about life on the neck generations ago.

When people visit the neck today, the common first impression is "Wow. You have to go a long way to do your grocery shopping." Or "You probably don't go out to eat in restaurants much when you live down here, do you?"

Such comments bring a chuckle from the group seated around Anne Sterling's dining room table. When they were growing up in the decade encompassing World War II, most necks were still operating on a barter economy. You took eggs, milk, and butter from the farm to the store and traded for coffee and sugar. "People didn't have much money in those days, but no one considered themselves poor," said Trissie.

"People grew what they needed on the farm, and they caught fish and crabs in the summer and shot ducks and geese in the winter," said Nancy. "I remember my granddaddy going out at night and coming home with a tub full of black ducks, and I had to get up and clean them. But my, they were good. Corn-fed black ducks. It doesn't get any better."

Nancy grew up in Craddock Neck's "outermost house." If you look at a topo map of the neck, a single black square sits at the very tip of a swath of green. The green represents the extent of the high land, and the black square represents the house Nancy grew up in. It is remote.

"No one threw anything away," said Jo Sue. "When they butchered a chicken they saved the feet, trimmed off the nails, and boiled them in a pot. Chewed the meat off the bones."

"I knew a woman who used to eat the head," said Trissie.

"People didn't go out to restaurants," said Nancy "We would take eggs and butter and maybe a chicken to the store and get other things in return. If we were lucky, we might get a hot dog. Momma and Daddy would share one and give me a whole one."

"They had movies in Belle Haven and Exmore, and now and then we would go to the movies on a Saturday night. It was always a western. Either Roy Rogers or Gene Autry," said Jo Sue.

"People had family dinners," said Anne. "We would go down the neck nearly every Sunday after church to have dinner with family."

Anne's parents moved to Shields when she was a child, but she spent as much time as she could down the neck. "Every summer I went down the neck and stayed with my grandparents, I just loved it. The roads weren't paved and they didn't have electricity, but it was like Heaven to me."

"I remember when they put in electricity," said Trissie. "It was the most wonderful thing. The only problem was, they put the poles right in the middle of the field and every time you worked the field you would have to go around the poles. But nobody complained. We were glad to get it."

Exmore was a thriving railroad town in those days, with shops offering the latest fashions from Baltimore, but during the austere years of the world war, the people of the neck often made their own.

"Do you remember having dresses made out of flour sacks?"

"That I do."

People who lived in the necks of the Eastern Shore were like family, even to the point of handing down clothes.

"Anne's momma knitted her the prettiest red sweater," said Jo Sue. "Anne was just beautiful when she was wearing it, and I liked it so much."

Jo Sue is a few years younger than Anne, and she had a feeling that when Anne outgrew that sweater, it might be coming her way.

"When my momma got that sweater she decided to sew some suede elbow patches on the sleeves, like on the sport coats men wear. That just ruined it. It was so pretty when Anne had it. I vowed I would never wear anything with elbow patches again," she laughed.

A childhood on Craddock Neck forms bonds that last a lifetime, between individuals and families. Anne's father, John Drewer, and Jo Sue's father, Harry W. Drummond, farmed together, and later, with Walter Drummond, formed H.W. Drummond, Inc. a retailer of heating oil and auto parts. John Drewer concentrated on farming and Harry Drummond operated the retail business. Walter Drummond sold out to the other two partners and died early in life. H.W. Drummond, Inc. today is still a very successful supplier of oil and auto parts on the Eastern Shore.

Craddock was one of the first necks in Accomack County to have a school. In 1798 James and Anah Hornsby donated land to the trustees of the Craddock and Occohannock Academy. The school operated on and off for a number of years.

Craddock Neck also had its military heroes. Albert Smith and John Killmon, Jr. were sons of Craddock Neck. Clinton Johnson lived in Belle Haven, but his mother lived in Craddock Neck. All three were killed during the waning years of World War II.

George Boggs's father was a tenant farmer in Craddock Neck, working the Drummond farm on the creek where Bill Sterling and a number of his relatives live today. George was born in 1930 and remembers playing with the children in the neighborhood. The fact that George is black and most of his neighbors white seemed to make little difference. "We all got along great and have been friends for many years," he says. "I had a pet goat and a little cart, and I would hitch up the goat, pull his tail, and he would take off. We were like everyone else. We fished and hunted and Daddy had a big garden. He grew potatoes, watermelon, cantaloupes, tomatoes, most everything. We had hogs and would have hog killing in the winter. We didn't have much money, but no one did in those days. Nobody went hungry in the neck, though."

The difference between George's family and those of most neighbors was that the others owned the home they lived in and the land they worked. George's family were tenants, and the property was not their own. "My Momma said all her life that all she wanted was a place of her own, her own home. I saw to it that she got it."

George went to school in a red, four-room schoolhouse in Craddockville, walking through the woods from his home, a hike of about two miles. George was an athlete, and even now at age 93 is tall and lean and agile. In the summers he traveled to Atlantic City, New Jersey, working at one of the food shops on the Boardwalk to make some cash to send back home. After graduation from school, George enlisted in the Army and after basic training and weapons school was sent to Korea and assigned to a company of riflemen. He saw action in the battle for Pork Chop Hill, one of the bloodiest of the war. A film, *Pork Chop Hill*, made in 1953, documented the battle. It starred Gregory Peck and Rip Torn.

George went to vocational school on the GI Bill after being discharged, opened a four-chair beauty salon in Philadelphia, married, and became a successful businessman, running the salon and managing properties owned by his father-in-law in Philadelphia. But George maintained a close relationship with friends and relatives on the Shore, visiting often to see his mother. Eventually, he was able to buy a house for her in Craddockville, had it renovated, and moved her in. At age 78, George's mom finally had a place to call her own.

George becomes emotional when talking about Mattie Sarah Boggs, his mother, and now and then he pauses to wipe away a tear. "Mom raised five kids and taught us a set of values to live by, how to treat people, to be kind, generous. She loved everyone. She dressed us up and took us to church every Sunday. We didn't have a car, but we would start off on Craddockville Road on foot, and someone would always pick us up and give us a ride. Everyone in the neck knew us."

George's mother passed away in 1984, but he still has the bungalow in Craddockville where she lived, and he stays there during frequent visits to the Shore from Philadelphia.

Like most necks, Craddock has its share of tales, some taller than others, but all eminently believable. Jim Smith remembers Ellis Drummond, an oysterman who caused the wreck of a steamboat in Craddock Creek. Ellis was a strong, athletic man, and he made himself a pair of stilts and entertained the kids of the neck by walking around towering above everyone else. Ellis got the idea that he could put the stilts to more practical use in his line of work. So, when he was out working his oyster ground one day he brought along the stilts and found that they helped him explore much deeper water, discovering oysters he normally would not have found.

While Ellis was foraging for oysters along a fairly deep channel, a steamboat entered the creek, and the captain saw Ellis standing knee-deep in what the captain had thought was the channel. Fearing he was about to run aground, the captain made a sharp turn to the port side, and was soon grounded on a mud flat for the remainder of the day.

And finally, this brings us to the story about Rev. Thomas Teackle's home, a fire on a cold, dark night in the winter of 1778, and the birth of a legend that has existed for nearly two-and-a-half centuries. The story of the Yahoo of Craddock Neck.

The Yahoo of Craddock Neck

On a dark night during the winter of 1778 a plantation house in the heart of Craddock Neck was burned to the ground, reportedly by British soldiers. The house was once owned by the Reverend Thomas Teackle, a noted figure during the colonial period of the Eastern Shore. Rev. Teackle was an Anglican minister who served the Shore for forty years and was the first rector of what became St. George's Church in Pungoteague.

Rev. Teackle was a highly respected member of the clergy, but, unfortunately, he is remembered prominently as being accused by Col. Edmund Scarburgh of having an illicit relationship with Edmund's wife, Mary.

The reverend was charged with fornication, but the charges were never processed, and he gradually regained his position of respect in the community. It turned out that Scarburgh's accusation was a ruse, part of an elaborate plot to dump his wife in favor of a younger woman named Anne Toft. (See "Sex and Violence in Gargathy Neck")

So, the house that was reduced to ashes on that night in 1778 held something of an exalted position among the people who lived in the neck. It had been the historic home of the first pastor of their church. Later, a new two-story frame home with brick ends was built on the Teackle Farm. The home later became known as Currituck, or Craddock.

To celebrate the new construction, the family that owned the home invited everyone to a housewarming party. Oysters were roasted, black ducks and brant were grilled over coals, and the ale freely flowed.

All was merry until late that evening when someone heard a strange sound outside. A group quickly gathered on the lawn and listened intently. Suddenly, there was an eerie shriek and then a series of sharp, animal-like calls that seemed to come from the marsh.

"Yahoo! Yahoo!"

All was quiet for a few moments, and then it happened again.

"Yahoo! Yahoo!"

Needless to say, the party was over, but at dawn the next day the men of the neck gathered at the Teackle Farm. Some were on horseback, others on foot. Most of them were armed with either a shotgun or pistol. They spread out and spent the day searching the woods and marsh, but they found nothing. There was no evidence of either man or beast. They searched again a day later. No luck. They searched at night using torchlights to shine in the creature's eyes. No luck.

After a few weeks the men stopped searching and things got back to normal, although conversations around the dinner table frequently centered on the mysterious creature that became known as the "Yahoo of Craddock Neck."

Within a few months it probably would have been forgotten, but it happened again near a farm some distance from the Teackle place. Again, a search was carried out. Again, nothing was found. Encounters with the Yahoo went on sporadically for years, usually occurring in the spring.

The Craddock Neck Yahoo has become part of Eastern Shore history and folklore. Ralph T. Whitelaw wrote of the creature in his history *Virginia's Eastern Shore*. Whitelaw speculated that the creature "could be a non-native aquatic animal that comes to the area periodically to breed or feed."

Thomas Teackle Upshur, a well-known Eastern Shore historian and genealogist, spoke of the Yahoo during the dedication ceremony for the new county court house in Accomac in 1900.

Jennings C. Wise, in *Ye Kingdome of Accawmacke* (1911) wrote, "This bogey, whatever it may be, whether man or beast, has been sought by armed hunting parties for several centuries. By day and by torchlight, its trail of foot-tracks has been followed only to be lost as the weird cry of "Yahoo! Yahoo!" sounds through the dismal wastes of marsh to warn the curious of the futility of their quest, and to make the blood of the half-hearted searchers run cold."

While most of the accounts of the Yahoo are second-hand affairs coming from persons who have never actually heard the creature in the wild, we do have one written by an eye (ear?) witness. Captain Jack Melson lived on the Teackle Farm and on February 16, 1957 dictated the following account to Mary Easley. The story is published in *High Tide in Jackie's Kitchen*, a cookbook written by the captain's daughter, Jackie Farlow.

> It was the greatest thing ever came across me! I was going across the marsh one day. I was driving a horse cart. When I got over there, I heard a peculiar noise. Sounded like someone driving a pole in the water. Thought it was Captain Fred Harrison, but further I got down there, the noise was further to my left. I came to the conclusion it was not Captain Fred so I kept on down. When I got to the bay shore, I stopped the horse and the fuss was coming out the marsh. I listened to it and could not tell to save my life what it was, and I have never known what it was. I drove on to where the noise was and then it stopped. This was the first time I ever heard it, probably 35 years ago.

Then, you could hear it most every year, and I never could find out what it was. Sometime you would think it was one thing. Thought it could be a muskrat but never heard it where other muskrats or other animals were, and I never heard it anywhere else.

On one occasion, Omar Kellam and I went down and we heard the sound or fuss calling in the marsh. I said "Let's go and see if we can find that thing." So I got out close to the noise, close as to that puppy (which was under my feet). I looked with all my eyes and I had my gun with me, and I shot right where I heard the noise and it shut right up and I never heard it any more.

It has a funny sound. Has about three different sounds to it. Had some funny experiences with the thing. One time I wanted to go somewhere, and I sent Johnnie on the marsh for something. Always heard it in the spring or summer – March to July. Johnnie went on there, and he heard that thing and he almost ran his toenails off. Ewell heard it too, and thought it would scare Johnnie and went to get him. I have not heard it for at least ten years.

Bobbie Melson, grandson, says at a distance the sound is like someone driving a fish pole in water, but near it it has three distinct chirps, then goes back to sounding like a pole being driven. Says grandfather is getting deaf. Has not heard it for ages but has been down to look for it.

The Bennett Brothers and the Blockade Runners of Hacks Neck

They say Jim Bennett could move like a shadow in the nightime forest, never seen and never heard, but always delivering the goods. Jim Bennett and his brothers were blockade runners in Hacks Neck during the Civil War. They started running shortly after Federal troops moved south from Newtown in November 1861, and then spread out over the bayside ports and wharves to block local shippers from sending goods to the western shore.

They kept at it for the duration of the war, until General Robert E. Lee surrendered at Appomattox Court House on 9 April 1865. On 3 June 1865 Jim Bennett walked into the office of Captain William B. Brokaw at the federal army headquarters in Pungoteague with his hat in his hand. "I hear that General Lee has surrendered," he said. "I reckon I ought to do the same."

Jim Bennett, over a period of about four years, made countless trips from the marshes of Hacks Neck across the bay to Mathews, Mobjack Bay, Gloucester County, Gwynn's Island – wherever he could find willing buyers hiding in a swamp that was as dark and remote as Hacks Neck.

Jim was in the smuggling business with two of his brothers, John, the eldest, and Teakle, who was a few years younger than Jim. Over the years, John and Teakle got caught and did jail time, but Jim never saw the inside of a prison. When Lee surrendered, Jim Bennett was on the Union's most wanted list, and he was wanted dead or alive.

While the Eastern Shore was not the focus of significant battles during the war, the two counties were very much involved in a more subtle form of warfare called blockade running. Beginning soon after the first shots were fired at Fort Sumter in April 1861, the Union began Project Anaconda, a plan to systematically strangle the South by closing its ports and denying the shipment of materials to support the war effort. On April 19 President Lincoln signed a proclamation ordering the blockade of southern ports, and on May 1 Captain Silas Horton Stringham took command of a flotilla of gunboats, charged with shutting down ports from Alexandria, Virginia to Key West, Florida.

During the early days of the blockade, the anaconda more closely resembled a slimy eel than a constricting snake. Potential victims routinely slithered from its grasp, or avoided it entirely. As the war wore on, both sides devoted much of their resources to sea power. Secretary of the Navy Gideon Welles oversaw the construction of a large navy powered by steam, and by the war's end the United States possessed one of the largest and most powerful navies in the world. By early 1862 most of the operational ports along the North Carolina and Virginia coast were under blockade by the Union navy.

The blockade project was the main reason the Union army moved quickly to occupy Virginia's Eastern Shore. It gave the northern forces a beachhead in the Chesapeake Bay area that was crucial to shipping. It was the perfect venue to monitor and enforce the coming and going of ships. They might not have predicted that Eastern Shore men and women would band together in a ragtag navy to wage guerilla warfare for four years.

The war at sea had many implications. In the larger picture, it affected international trade. England needed cotton grown in the Confederate south. The south needed arms, gunpowder, and military and medical supplies. The Union built a navy of fast-moving steamships designed for open water. The South built low-profile, shallow-draft vessels designed to avoid detection. The goal of the south was to keep its army supplied by avoiding the blockade. The goal of the Union was to prevent the shipment of arms and other military support, and to shrink the range of areas along the southern coast where shipments could enter.

The Bennett Brothers and the Blockade Runners of Hacks Neck

While the Union navy patrolled the waterways, it was the army that maintained the blockade on land by preventing coastal residents from using private vessels to aid the enemy on distant battlefields. Although the Eastern Shore saw no major battles during the war, constant skirmishes were going on between army troops and the "Hacks Neck Navy." Although blood was seldom shed, written accounts indicate that some of the more active blockade runners would have faced execution if they had been caught. Jim Bennett was no doubt one of these. Lower-level blockade runners were usually fined and/or given jail time, and their boats and other equipment destroyed or confiscated.

Jim Bennett was something of a Robin Hood figure in Hacks Neck, making probably hundreds of trips across the bay to provide goods to support the Confederacy, and he was one of very few known blockade runners on the Shore never to have been caught. He was a skillful sailor, a man with pedigree linked to the sea. His grandfather, Captain William Bennett, was a master sailor with the Virginia Navy during the Revolutionary War. Bennett's close calls were what established his legend, and no doubt some of the Bennett stories, like those of Robin Hood, have been improved and embellished in many re-tellings.

Most involve narrow escapes as Federal troops closed in, usually by exiting by a rear window or wearing a clever disguise. On one occasion the troops entered a home where Bennett was staying. As the owner stalled them, Bennett jumped out of a rear window, sprinted to Butcher Creek, and swam underwater to safety on the other side.

The assistant provost marshal at Drummondtown thought he had Bennett cornered one night in October 1864. But Bennett out-foxed the marshal and fifteen of his troops. The provost marshal wrote the following report to his superior, Lt. Col Frank White, in Eastville:

> I received information that James Bennett, the celebrated blockade runner, was on the Shore. I at once employed as a detective a man named Martin Laws, who was formerly engaged in the business. I received from him information that on Wednesday night last Bennett would be at one of three houses near Pungoteague

With about fifteen men I started to the (John Stevens) house named, taking my detective with me as a guide.... I found the house on a neck of land about six miles distant from Pungoteague. Arriving there about three a.m...the Sergeant first went to the door, it was opened by Stevens and was shown in; he found a woman in bed and was informed that it was Stevens's wife. He inquired whether there was anyone else in the house and was answered in the negative.

A search was then proposed, when the woman said there were two men upstairs, but there was no harm about them; that their names were Jim Stevens and Sammy Kimble. She was ordered to go up and wake them, and did so. Some time elapsed and they didn't come down, when she went again, and coming down the stairs following her and the light went out, when she said there was not a candle in the house, but afterwards got one without any delay; when the light was struck, both men went to the door as if to go out, but upon being stopped, both expressed an entire willingness to stay, so much so as to throw the sergeant off his guard, and when a few minutes afterwards they said they wished to go to attend to call of nature, he allowed them to do so, only sending one man with each.

One of them carried in his hand a shawl and upon getting to the fence, he jumped it and called to the other, 'John. Come on,' which John started to do but was caught by the man in charge of him; the other man, however, got some distance start, and before the guard could get his pistol (it being under his coat), he was some 25 or 30 yards away from him. The guard fired at him with what effect is not known, as he succeeded in getting into the woods and escaping.

When I got to the house Laws told me the man was Jim Bennett but he did not know how he came into his house. He answers the description of him in every way, wears his beard the same way, and is like him in all other respects. The other man gave his name as John Riley; says he came from Maryland, and has not the slightest idea as to how the other man got into bed with him.... Riley now says that after he saw Bennett downstairs he did not recognize him as any one he had ever seen. When the woman went upstairs, she stayed a long time talking with the men in an undertone and had a light with her. The answers given to me by the proprietor of the house were so conflicting that I arrested him, and of course arrested Riley as an accomplice of Bennett's.

"I now forward them to you. I am of the opinion I will yet succeed in catching him (Bennett)."

James E. Mears in 1951 compiled a lengthy narrative titled *The Eastern Shore During the War of Secession Period and Reconstruction*. The narrative was not published, but bound copies were donated to the governments of both counties and the Library of Virginia. The account of Bennett's escape is included in that narrative. Mears was also the author of *Hacks Neck and its People – Past and Present*, and portions of the Civil War narrative were included in that book as well. In it, Mears wrote that federal troops were given orders to shoot blockade runners, rebel spies, and rebel mail carriers if caught in the act of delivering mail to or from the rebel lines.

> Blockade running was carried on by certain residents of the Virginia Eastern Shore from early in the war until virtually its end, despite the continuous and zealous efforts of the Federal army of occupation to break it up. (Lt. Col. Frank) White, commanding the Federal forces on the Virginia Eastern Shore, on May 9, 1864, from Eastville, issued an order that "provost guards shoot wherever found blockade runners, if taken in the act of conveying goods to the rebel lines; rebel spies, if found arriving and in concealment within our lines; rebel mail carriers, if taken in the act of conveying mail to or from the rebel lines."

Hacks Neck was not the only coastal community on the Shore to harbor blockade runners, but the geography of Hacks Neck made it ideal. Hacks Neck is a huge wedge of forest and swampland, and it is threaded by many shallow, narrow creeks and guts, offering many options for someone wishing to stash a small boat. The neck is a marshy, soggy equilateral triangle. The apex of the triangle lies near the village of Pungoteague. Just north of town the Taylor Creek branch of Pungoteague Creek drains a small cypress swamp near St. George's and St. Paul's churches. Just south of town Nandua Creek peters out near the intersection of Big Pine Road and Rt. 178. From this axis the ragged margins of the neck run for about eight miles to the Chesapeake Bay. The third side of the triangle runs along beach and marsh for eight more miles to make a geometric completion.

Hacks Neck, of course, is not a perfect triangle. It is perforated by Buckland Gut, Hancock Gut, Horse Hole Creek, and Butcher Creek, among unnamed others. If someone wanted to hide a 20-foot skiff, fill it with contraband, and head out some moonless night for the western shore, Hacks Neck offered many options, including secluded forest trails linking mooring sites with stores, farms, and other suppliers of goods that would go to customers across the bay on a late-night supply run. The creeks, guts, back roads, and forest trails were well known to locals. To Union army enlisted men, they might well have been wilderness.

Blockade runners had varying reasons for getting involved in this dangerous, uncomfortable business. Some were motivated by patriotism, others by profiteering. Many local people stood with the Confederacy, and they had friends and family who had crossed the bay and signed up to fight for the cause. For others, it was a matter of business. Blockades create shortages of goods people need to survive. When things are in short supply, the value goes up, and prices become inflated. If someone knows the backwoods and is comfortable navigating in the darkness, and is willing to face the music if caught, then there is good money to be made.

For local planters, running the blockade was necessary to get their crop to the market, to recoup their investment. Local runners did not often deal in gunpowder and weapons, but more likely in cornmeal, oats, leather goods, clothing, shoes, salted pork, clams and oysters, and peach brandy. In other words, it was the usual shipment of goods that had always been sent to market, until the Union blockade attempted to end it. The weapons and gunpowder were usually supplied by ocean-going ships, often from foreign countries.

The boats used for blockade running on the Shore were mostly skiffs around twenty feet long, with a shallow draft for negotiating local creeks and guts, but sufficiently seaworthy to withstand the open waters of the bay. The boats were usually kept at the heads of narrow, shallow waterways and often had plugs installed in the bottoms so they could be sunk in the shallow water where they were hidden. When the time came to make a run, the boats would be pulled onto land, drained, the plugs inserted, and then loaded for the trip. The masts were removed and hidden in the woods, or sometimes used as fence rails. and the sails were hidden in the homes, often folded and used in baby cribs. While blockade running at sea was a large-scale operation, activities on the Shore more closely resembled guerilla warfare, with limited operations usually undertaken at night or in poor weather conditions. Writes Mears:

> Those who engaged in blockade running usually crossed the Chesapeake in small canoes when the nights were dark and weather conditions such that they were less likely to be intercepted by the blockading fleet of the U.S. Navy. Despite the fact that stormy weather was commonly the lot of these daring and intrepid men, not many of whom possessed even a compass, this writer has heard of or seen nothing to indicate that any of them was drowned on such a mission. While nearly all of them eventually were taken into custody, there were few instances where it occurred while in the act of running the blockade. The small boats used for these voyages, when not in use, usually were sunk in some out of the way gut, and the sails were sometimes placed in cribs in which babies slept, because the soldiers frequently made an inspection of premises occupied by suspected runners. As a further deterrent, the Federals required all sailing craft to be licensed and such were not permitted to leave or enter a creek between sunset and sunrise.

The hazard of getting the goods to the boats was almost as great as getting them across the bay. Soldiers patrolled the roads both day and night, making it necessary for the supplies to be taken at night through woods and over trails that often ran as far east as the seaside. When the bayside necks were reached, the contraband was hidden in houses, woods, or marshes until weather conditions were suitable for the bay crossing.

Merchants suspected of supplying blockade runners often were forced out of business. Mears writes that Cornelius T. Taylor, who kept a store at Pungoteague in the early years of the war, was forced to close. "General Lockwood, in a letter from Drummondtown, dated November 27, 1863, protesting the appointment of Cornelius T. Taylor as postmaster at Pungoteague, made during Lockwood's temporary absence at Harper's Ferry during the previous summer, said: 'I regard Mr. Taylor at Pungoteague so deeply implicated in attempting to run the blockade that I closed his store more than a year ago.'" (Lockwood's Letters in National Archives).

According to Mears, the very small boats used in blockade running, as well as the difficulty of eluding the Federal troops on the Eastern Shore, restricted the size and quantity of the goods. "Nathaniel J.W. LeCato of lower Accomack, who was a cavalry company captain in the 39th (Eastern Shore) Regiment of Virginia Volunteers, in his novel, *Tom Burton or the Days of 1861*, published in 1888, says about blockade running: 'There was money in whiskey and medicine, especially in quinine, which was in great demand for the Southern army...' and that many Eastern Shore people' had friends and relatives on the other side, and were in almost weekly communication with them by means of blockade running, which was carried on extensively on account of the large profits it offered to the hardy men engaged in it.'"

The legend of Jim Bennett and his brothers seems to have waned with the end of the war. Bennett's family had a small farm in Hacks Neck, and it is presumed he returned to life on the farm at the end of the war. There are few public records regarding his personal life. According to the MilesFiles, an online genealogical databank maintained by the Eastern Shore of Virginia Heritage Center (ESPL), Bennett had a large family. He was one of eleven children born to Covington (Covy) Bennett, Sr. and Margaret (Peggy) Caruthers Bennett. Jim was married three time, to Margaret Watson (1852), Rachel Shrieves (1868), and Elizabeth Mears (1887). He had six children each with Margaret and Rachel.

His grandfather was William Bennett (1744-1802), an orphan who was indentured to Arnold Morgan of Hacks Neck to learn the trade of carpentry. He became an officer in the Virginia Navy during the Revolution, serving on the ship *Deliverance*.

The few public records reveal little about Jim Bennett's life after the war. An item in the *Peninsula Enterprise*, a newspaper published in Accomac, reports that in November 1886 two men were arrested and convicted of stealing $3.60 from James H. Bennett.

The April 1890 term of court in Accomack shows that James H. Bennett was released from jail after being held for failure to pay two fines and the costs of prosecution.

The final mention came in the April 1903 proceedings of the Accomack County Court when an inquest into the death of James H. Bennett was requested by Levi Boggs, Justice of the Peace and Acting Coroner. Jim Bennett was dead at age 73, but his legend lives on.

And What Was the Cargo?

The cargo delivered by ocean-going blockade runners was not just guns and ammunition to aid the war effort. The blockade caused shortages of many of life's necessities, ranging from food and clothing to fancy liquors and musical instruments. This was true of both international shipments and those that originated on the Eastern Shore and made their way across the bay to fellow Virginians. Local blockade runners probably had little to offer in the way of weapons, but they had food and clothing, tools and hardware needed by planters.

There are no records of items shipped by local runners, but cargo manifests listing individual items on ocean-going ships have been found, and the variety is striking. Of course, even during times of war, commerce involved more than just armaments. Luxuries were always on the manifest lists. What follows are four manifests from blockade runners travelling from Bermuda to the Confederate states. These were found in the Custom House in the historic city of St. George's, Bermuda many years after the war. Bermuda and the Bahamas were good trading posts for blockade runners because of their location and because many of the residents supported the Confederacy.

These are from the website *Anchor*, a North Carolina history online resource. A *hogshead* is a large wooden barrel holding about 63 gallons. A *tierces* is a cask holding about 43 gallons.

The Ships and Their Cargo:

Minho, about 253 tons, St. George's for St. John's, N.B., September 26, 1862, F. T. Parke, master:

From steamer *Phebe*, England: 48 hogsheads brandy, 21 1/2 casks brandy, 63 cases brandy, 10 casks wine, 673 cases wine, 6 1/4 quarts whiskey, 14 hogsheads spirits, 8 cases apothecary ware, 1 case marine glasses, 1 case cutlery, 2 bales merchandise, 641 cases general merchandise, 7 cases quinine, 31 boxes candles, 5 cases drugs, 3 parcels thread, 8 packages merchandise (boots), 12 chests tea (from *Merrimac*), 1 case stationary, 12 cases mustard and starch, 37 barrels ale and porter, 6 barrels crushed sugar, 1 box sardines, 4 cases merchandise (meats), 14 kegs gunpowder, 2 cases merchandise, 5 cases tea, 1 case screws, 28 cases tin, 32 cases shoes.

Little Hattie, about 247 tons, St. George's for Nassau, June 30, 1864, Jesse DeHorsey, master:

200 sacks saltpeter, 15 casks hardware, 16 casks hardware, 6 casks hardware, 2 casks curry combs, 1 cask hardware, 4 casks steel, 1 case steel, 50 barrels provisions, 19 cases stationery, 11 cases stationery, 5 cases fluid, 1 case merchandise, 13 cases leather, 2 cases carbines, 1 case sabers, 21 cases merchandise, 8 cases cavalry equipment, 1 case merchandise, 6 bales twine, 1 roll rubber packing, 50 bales cartridge paper, 120 pigs lead, 6 bales bagging, 25 coils rope, 1 case merchandise, 6 bales shirts, 9 cases merchandise.

Princess Royal, about 103 tons, St. George's for Nassau, December 14, 1864, T. D. Newbold, master:

2 bales cotton waste, 2 cases cheese, 1 case fruit, 10 bags coffee, 46 cases oil, 81 bales bagging, 1 boat, 14 floats, 11 barrels porter, 1 barrel ale, 6 cases wine, 224 bundles, 356 plates, 107 sheets iron, 5 casks brandy, 5 rolls matting, 1 iron safe, 2 pianos, 2 boxes harmoniums, 25 cases merchandise, 173 barrels potatoes.

Pleiades, about 330 tons, St. George's for Nassau, December 20, 1864, William Knowlton, master:

From W. H. Gosling's stores (bonded September 6, 1864), imported per *Solway Queen*: 573 tierces beef, 745 barrels pork, 65 cases preserved vegetables, 125 cases preserved meats. From same store (bonded October 4, 1864), imported per *Emily Agnes*: 418 tierces beef, 400 barrels pork, 66 cases beef juice, 22 cases preserved soup, 9 cases preserved beef. From J. W. Mosson's warehouse (bonded October 4, 1864), imported per *Queen of Clippers*: 944 cases preserved meat. From same warehouse (bonded July 13, 1864), imported per *J. W.*: 196 cases vegetables.

Hoffman's Wharf and the Days of Guano

The opening of the railroad in 1884 and the formation of the Eastern Shore of Virginia Produce Exchange in 1900 marked the beginning of a new era in agriculture on the Eastern Shore. The railroad revolutionized transportation, and the Exchange made farmers think about marketing and producing crops of superior quality to get an edge over competitors. Almost overnight, farm products from the Eastern Shore were being marketed throughout the eastern United States and into Canada and Cuba.

The Eastern Shore's agricultural revolution was far reaching. It touched not only farmers and shippers and sales agents; it spawned an array of satellite industries. From 1900 through 1919 production of white potatoes in the two counties rose from 11,000 acres to 53,000 acres. Barrels were needed to get those potatoes to market, and most farming communities had at least one barrel factory.

To increase yields and grow a superior crop, farmers needed fertilizer, and much of it came from guano collected in the West Indies. Guano was made from the waste of birds and bats and was collected wherever there were nesting colonies. As droppings built up over time, they would be scraped up, packaged, and shipped to agricultural suppliers.

Crews, consisting mainly of black men, were being shipped out of coastal cities such as Baltimore and Norfolk to work on guano islands in the Caribbean. Shippers found that the guano trade was more profitable than hauling lumber, and the local men sent to dig the guano were paid $2 per day, not a bad wage back then.

The development of the guano industry accelerated on the Shore when technology was developed to manufacture guano directly from fish scraps, and local seafood dealers and other entrepreneurs were quick to capitalize on one of the Shore's most abundant natural resources: fish. Guano and fish oil factories were soon popping up on the seaside and the bayside.

Hacks Neck, with its easy access to the Chesapeake Bay, was a prime producer of guano. Court postings of the day were filled with applications from local dealers to operate fish traps and build plants for processing fish guano. Within a few years, two factories were operating on Cedar Island, and others were at Chincoteague, Assateague, and Tangier Island.

Hacks Neck had the largest guano fleet on the Shore. Powell and Morse & Co, (later incorporated as the American Fish Guano Company) built a factory on the harbor at Hoffman's Wharf (now Harborton), and had a fleet of ocean-going vessels ranging as far north as Maine. Most of the factories used menhaden, a small, oily fish common in the Chesapeake and on the seaside. The factory produced both fish oil, which was used in the manufacture of paint, cosmetics, and other products, and dried guano, which was used to fertilize crops.

Fish guano was marketed as containing all the nutrients of bird guano, but at a fraction of the cost. After all, guano was simply fish that had gone through the digestive process provided by the birds. Locally produced guano eliminated birds from the equation and came up with a more cost-effective product.

According to James E. Mears, the plant at Hoffman's Wharf was the idea of the Powell brothers, businessmen of Onancock, who decided to get into the menhaden industry and picked the wharf because of its proximity to deep water on Pungoteague Creek. The Powells were looking for someone to manage the business and consulted the owners of a plant on the western shore, who recommended a young man from

Hoffman's Wharf - Harborton

Connecticut named Albro J. Morse, who had been working for them. They hired Morse with the agreement that he would run the business, and if the business succeeded to the point where they paid off their investment and realized a profit, they would sell their shares to him and his associates.

Morse took over the business and operated it as the American Fish Guano Company until about 1900. It was subsequently operated by Connecticut owners under the name Menhaden Fish and Oil Company until about 1917, with Morse at the helm. The plant changed owners a number of times and finally went out of business around the time of World War II.

At its peak, the company owned a fleet of steam-powered fishing vessels that ranged along the coast in search of menhaden, which it brought back to Hoffman's Wharf for processing. According to Mears, the largest ship in the fleet was the *J.W. Hawkins*, which was 165 feet in length and had a capacity of 750,000 pounds of fish. The *Hawkins* sailed out of Hoffman's Wharf from 1892 to 1896. The *Hannah A. Lennon* was 112 feet long and could hold 600,000 pounds. She sailed from 1901 until 1917.

The plant employed about 200 people and processed an annual average catch of about 12 million pounds. The managers and supervisors of the plant lived in Hoffman's Wharf or the nearby area, but most of the laborers were seasonal workers who stayed in temporary housing and returned home at the end of the season.

The menhaden and guano industry brought prosperity to Hoffman's Wharf and to the neighboring Hacks Neck community. James Mears wrote of the Morse family that "probably no other family on the Eastern Shore of Virginia lived in greater elegance."

The Morse family established a private school for their children and permitted children of the community to enroll. "They had horses, carriages, a coachman and other servants, a well-stocked 'wine cellar,' they entertained elaborately, traveled much and Mr. Morse was a member of select and expensive clubs in the northern cities," wrote Mears.

The industry at Hoffman's Wharf brought many improvements to Hacks Neck. The first telephone line on the Eastern Shore was constructed in 1894 linking the wharf to the railroad station in Keller by way of Pungoteague. Its promoter was Albro J. Morse, who needed telephone lines to connect his business with telegraph services at the Keller station. He and other local business owners organized the Peninsula Telephone Company in the spring of 1894 with its main office at Harborton.

In 1894 the name Hoffman's Wharf was changed to Harborton at the suggestion of Morse, because at the time there was a community elsewhere in Virginia called Hoffmans, and mail was frequently delayed because of confusion.

The post office was opened in Hacks Neck in 1872 and was located at Hoffman's Wharf, situated in the store operated by Hoffman and Walker. The Hacks Neck post office, in western Hacks Neck between Butcher Creek and Nandua Creek, opened around 1910. One of the early postmasters was Thomas Henry Bennett, who operated the post office in his store. According to the MilesFiles, Thomas Henry Bennett was the younger brother of Jim Bennett, the noted blockade runner of Hacks Neck.

The Bennett Brothers and the Blockade Runners of Hacks Neck

Saturday Afternoons in Pungoteague

Along with Drummondtown and Eastville, the two county seats, Pungoteague was one of the more bustling communities of the Eastern Shore. In fact, court was held in Pungoteague during the early years, but was moved to Drummondtown (Accomac) to better serve settlers who were populating the northern section of the county.

Pungoteague was on the main stage coach road connecting bay-side communities such as Guilford, Onancock, Belle Haven, Hadlock, Franktown, Bridgetown, Shadyside, Eastville, and Cherrystone Wharf. Pungoteague was the head of Hacks Neck, which was named for Dr. George Hack, a German physician who came to the area around 1650 when was about 38 years old. He patented 400 acres in 1650, and was granted 1350 more in 1659 for transporting 27 individuals to the county.

Before the railroad era, Pungoteague was a community where people gathered to do business, socialize, shop, and perhaps enjoy a pint of good cheer. The first play performed in North America debuted in Pungoteague. *Ye Beare and Ye Cubb* was a political satire that poked fun of the English establishment, and it resulted in the arrest of the performers.

While "court day" was an occasion for local residents to gather in the two county seats, Saturday was the day for socializing in Pungoteague.

James Mears grew up in Hacks Neck and in 1937 published a book about the neck called *Hacks Neck and its People – Both Past and Present*. Mr. Mears was a prolific writer, and in 1957 he assembled a collection of writings on the Civil War and Reconstruction titled *The Eastern Shore During the War of Secession Period and Reconstruction*. The collection consisted of typed pages, double spaced, hand laid in cardboard bindings, and each volume was about three inches thick. Copies were given to the local governments and to the Library of Virginia. A copy is in the collection of the Eastern Shore of Virginia Heritage Center (ESPL) in Parksley.

These writings, along with many years of columns published in *The Eastern Shore News*, provide a vivid portrait of the Eastern Shore in the nineteenth and twentieth centuries. Eastern Shore historian Brooks Miles Barnes says that Mears's research is invaluable to scholars today. "Mears's contribution to Eastern Shore history is surpassed by no one, including (Susie M.) Ames and (Ralph T.) Whitelaw," says Barnes. "Consulting his work is a must for anyone studying the nineteenth and twentieth centuries."

Mears grew up in Pungoteague and when he was writing his memoirs in the 1930s the events of the 1890s seemed to be fresh in his mind. "When I was a boy – in the 1890s – going to Pungoteague on Saturday afternoon was almost a ritual; it was an event to which farm boys looked forward. If a man wished to meet, without previous appointment, an acquaintance living almost anywhere in the Pungoteague Magisterial District, west of the railroad, the chance of seeing him at Pungoteague on such an afternoon was good."

On a Saturday afternoon in Pungoteague you might find people from Hacks Neck, Harborton, Boggs Wharf, Bobtown, Keller, Painter, Mappsburg, Belle Haven, Davis Wharf, Scarburgh Neck, Craddockville, Pennyville, Nandua, and Cedar View. Mears said it was not uncommon to have one hundred or more people in town, discussing crops, politics, the economy, and world affairs. "Merchandise was purchased at the stores, the 'cup that cheers' was enjoyed by some, shoes were repaired (and made to measure), harnesses mended, horses were shoed, and often traded, seafood and wildfowl were huckstered, now and then farm or other property sold at auction, and during election years candidates were on hand seeking votes, and occasionally there were political speeches," wrote Mears. In earlier years, slaves were sometimes sold on Saturday afternoons in Pungoteague.

Saturday was also "warrant day," according to Mears. In spring, the commissioner of the revenue would come to town with a list of personal property assessments and present bills to the owners. In the fall, the county treasurer would make an appearance to collect the taxes, usually parking his buggy in the shade of a huge pine tree that grew

Pungoteague was the home of Fowlkes Tavern, believed to be the location of the first play performed in America.

at the intersection of what today is Rt. 178 and Big Pine Road. Local folks would stop by and take care of their annual tax bills.

But Pungoteague was the place to be on a Saturday afternoon whether you had business to conduct or not. "It was an opportunity to chat with friends and acquaintances, to hear the local news and gossip, and see what was going on," wrote Mears.

Little remains of James Mears's Pungoteague of 1890. The stores have closed and most of them have been demolished. The only gathering place now is the post office, which sits at the corner of Rt. 178 and Harborton Road. But if you look closely, if you slow down and look at the old homes in Pungoteague, you will see its link with the past. St. George's Church, the oldest on the Shore, still keeps vigil adjacent to the community cemetery not far from where Taylor Branch of Pungoteague Creek drains a cypress swamp. Next door is St. Paul's Church, for generations the spiritual home of the Black residents of Pungoteague and Hacks Neck.

Across Rt. 178, on the grounds of a farmhouse, is a sign marking the location of Fowlkes Tavern, the venue where *Ye Beare and Ye Cubb* was performed on August 27, 1665. Kirk Mariner wrote in his book *Off 13* that William Darby, the writer, director, and lead actor of the play was arrested on the spot, along with his assistants, Cornelius Watkinson and Philip Howard. The three men were jailed and held until the next court session, but when the play was presented before the court, the justices ruled that nothing indecent had occurred. They ordered John Martin, who had brought charges against the three, to pay all court costs, including the board for Darby while he was in jail.

There still is drama to be found in Hacks Neck, if you know where to look.

Savage Neck Dunes

The tallest point on Virginia's Eastern Shore, towering more than fifty feet above sea level, is a sandy ridge running along the Chesapeake Bay south of Eastville. When it comes to geological features, the Eastern Shore tends to be understated: Lots of woods and farm fields, wide salt marshes, shallow bays, and low-slung barrier islands. But stand here on this ridge, look down the cliff edge where the dune spills abruptly into a loblolly pine forest, and the landscape becomes anything but subtle.

These dunes, which geologists believe may be more than 10,000 years old, are one of the more emphatic features of Savage Neck Dunes Natural Area Preserve, which was established in the late 1990s by the Virginia Department of Conservation and Recreation (DCR). These rare ancient dunes, and the plants associated with them, are one of the reasons the state gave the site such a high priority for protection.

The other reason is a bit less dramatic and obvious. A trail crosses the dune ridge and emerges onto a sandy beach on the Chesapeake Bay. Here, burrowing in the sand, is a tiny beetle that has a lot of clout within the scientific community. The northeastern beach tiger beetle (*Cicindela dorsalis dorsalis*) was once abundant along the northeast coast from Massachusetts to New Jersey as well as along the Chesapeake Bay. But the tiger beetle depends upon undisturbed beach habitat for its survival, and over the past two centuries we have left very little of our northeastern beaches undisturbed. Consequently, only two populations of the beetle remain on the barrier islands of our northeast coast, along with a more stable colony along the

Savage Neck Dunes

Chesapeake Bay, and that can be found here on the beach at Savage Neck.

The tiger beetle is on the federally threatened list, and Savage Neck Dunes has one of the largest populations remaining. The tiger beetles spend most of their lives as larvae living in burrows four to eight inches deep between the high tide line and the primary dunes. When the weather warms in June the adult insects will emerge, spend the summer foraging for food that the high tide brings in, and then breed and die. In late summer the eggs will hatch, larvae will again burrow into the sand, and the next generation will again await the coming summer.

The plight of the northeastern beach tiger beetle is emblematic of what happens when humans monkey around with natural systems. Beaches and similar coastal ecosystems are particularly vulnerable, both because of their fragility and their desirability. People want to live on the water, and we want easy and unlimited access to the beach. As our northeastern beaches lose their namesake bug, sanctuaries like Savage Neck Dunes become even more vital.

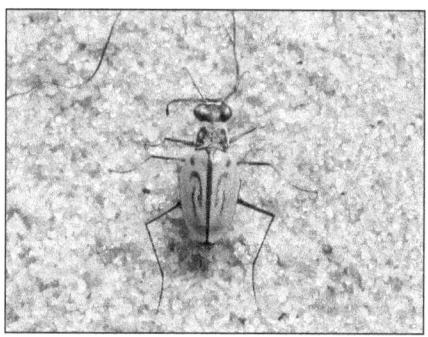

Tiger beetle

Savage Neck Dunes has plant communities that, like the tiger beetle, once were common along the coast, but in the past century or so, as natural dunes have been altered, they have become increasingly rare. A dune system can be a harsh environment, and not just any plant can survive there. The dunes are just a short distance from the Chesapeake Bay and are subject to salt laden breezes, occasional storm tides,

Tiger beetles mating

and sometimes strong onshore winds. An unusual group of plants has adapted well to these conditions and they make up a community of plants that are dependent upon each other for their survival. Some of the plants, such as salt meadow hay (*Spartina patens*), are more commonly found in tidal wetlands. Others, such as beach bean (*Strophostyles helvola*) and Carolina thistle (*Salsola kali*), thrive in arid environments. Perhaps the reason Savage Neck Dunes has such a diverse plant community is because the dunes are both arid and subject to occasional infusions of salt water.

The plants of the dunes could be called the architectural superstructure that holds the dunes together. Below the surface of the sand, roots and rhizomes of American beach grass (*Ammophila breviligulata*) and panic grass (*Panicum amarum amarulum*) provide a framework for the sand to build around. And on the surface of the dunes, low growing spurges such as seaside sandmat (*Chamaesyce polygonigolia*) trap sand carried by the breeze and hold it in place on the dune surface.

Here we have the ultimate symbiotic relationship. The dunes survive because the plants are there, and the plant community survives because of the dunes. Few natural dune grassland communities survive anymore, and once they are gone, they are difficult to regain. Sometimes dunes are lost to residential or recreational development, and frequently they are lost because of our need to stop beach erosion. Beaches are made of sand and they move readily with tides and wind, and the fact that the sea level is rising does not help. When communities invest millions of dollars in infrastructure, they want a sense of permanence that a migrating beach does not afford. That is usually when the bulldozers appear and the beach replenishment begins.

The dunes at Savage Neck have never felt the blade of a bulldozer. Instead, American beach grass and panic grass are sending roots and rhizomes into the core of the dune. Seaside sandmat and beach heather trap blowing sand particles. Sand builds up around sprouting saltmeadow hay. And farther upland grow wild black cherry, sweet gum, loblolly pine, and wax myrtle. All help anchor the dunes and protect the integrity of the system. These dunes have been here for hundreds, perhaps thousands, of years. Not exactly in the same spot, perhaps, but here nonetheless.

Once a dune system loses this natural balance of sand and structure, it likely is gone for good. Many of Virginia's coastal beaches, including Assateague Island National Seashore, are manipulated by machines, which re-build parking areas after storms and push up temporary protective dune lines to await the next storm.

Savage Neck Dunes became the property of the state in the late 1990s when two adjoining farms were purchased to create a preserve of nearly 300 acres, with a mile of beach frontage. Access to the dunes and the beach is via a hiking trail that begins in a small parking lot on Savage Neck Road, about two miles west of Eastville. The trail runs alongside a farm field that is being converted to grassland and scrubland. It then enters a loblolly pine forest and passes Custis Pond, a natural freshwater pond that geologists believe was part of an old coastal dune system. Once the trail enters the woods the footing gradually goes from hard-packed clay to loose sand as it nears the dunes. The pines become a bit stunted, and as the dunes become larger some of the trees appear to have limbs unnaturally close to the ground. In the dunes, the forest is an open canopy woodland consisting mainly of pines, sassafras, wild black cherry, and eastern red cedar. These secondary dunes are more than 50 feet tall, and in some places the dunes drop off steeply into the pine forest below. A smaller ridge of primary dunes separates the secondary dunes and the forest from the beach.

In less than a mile, the trail passes through grassland and scrub, pine forest, freshwater wetlands, maritime dunes, beach, and finally open bay. This diversity of habitat can provide some spectacular wildlife watching. The forest is part of a wooded migratory corridor used by songbirds as they move up and down the coast, and the bay and Custis Pond have waterfowl, shorebirds, gulls, and terns. So on a given day at Savage Neck Dunes you could see anything from a Northern Gannet to a Prothonotary Warbler. In addition, Savage Neck Dunes supports a varied community of mammals. Fox tracks are easily seen all along the sandy dunes, and in a sheltered valley between two large dunes fox dens are cut through the sand and into the subsoil. Raccoons are often seen foraging along the beach, and deer are plentiful in the forest and fields.

On a recent trip to Savage Neck, I met a visitor from Virginia Beach who was leaving the preserve as I arrived. Assuming I was a first-time visitor, he gave me a lengthy description of the preserve and told me what a wonderful place it was. "What we have here," he exclaimed, "is a good example of the government doing something right."

Following the Water on Joynes Neck

I once wrote a magazine profile on a naturalist named John K. Terres. John was an expert birder, a prolific writer, and editor of *Audubon* magazine for many years. Before computer software and web sites such as Merlin came along, most people used books to identify birds and study their habits and distribution. John wrote the *Audubon Society Encyclopedia of North American Birds*, which was published by Alfred A. Knopf, Inc. in 1980, a monumental work that weighed in at more than ten pounds and exceeded 1100 pages in length. I interviewed John about the project for a story in a birding magazine and that interview sparked a friendship that lasted many years.

John and I got together fairly often, first at his home in New Jersey and later in North Carolina after he retired from the magazine and joined the faculty at his alma mater, UNC in Chapel Hill. I think he realized early on that when it came to studying the natural history of birds, the future was in software, not print. He groused about the many hours spent laboring on the encyclopedia and the meager return it yielded. I suggested he should have priced it by the pound.

John was not only a talented writer and editor, he was an excellent illustrator. In his New Jersey home were a dozen or more loose-leaf notebooks filled with field sketches of everything from birds in flight to mushrooms. Most naturalists head out with binoculars around their neck, or a camera, but John always had his sketch pad, and he would come home with not only drawings, but notes about habitat, the weather, and the seasons.

I greatly admired this and decided to buy a sketchpad and pencils, develop my drawing skills, and take copious notes afield. I imagined myself, a few years down the road, having a collection of natural history field guides to complement my writing. The only problem is, I can't draw. John made it look easy, as simple as jotting down a sentence. I found the process intrusive, and I felt clumsy, looking around for a flat surface that might serve as a desk while I tried to sketch a chickadee.

So I gave the sketchpad and pencils to a friend and bought a tiny digital recorder. It slips easily into my shirt pocket, it weighs next to nothing, and it will record hours of what I call "audio sketches." It will even pick up the sounds of bird calls, so in the spring, when I hear a vaguely familiar song coming from a wooded thicket, I can record it and have Merlin come up with an ID. The software is amazingly accurate.

I like to record my notes rather than make sketches. I talk to myself when I am in the woods, and when I get home, I can relive the experience of being out there. I have spent a lot of time on a farm called Channel Point, which was owned by The Nature Conservancy and located near my home. TNC needed someone to keep an eye on the property and I needed a place where I could wander through the woods and talk to myself.

Channel Point is in Joynes Neck, east of the county seat of Accomac. Folly Creek makes up the southern boundary of the neck, beginning where Metompkin Inlet provides the flush valve for emptying the water behind Cedar and Metompkin Islands. Folly Creek heads west, makes a hard right, and winds its way through the mainland nearly to the town limits of Accomac. Many years ago, Accomac was known as Drummondtown, and Folly Creek was the usual route folks on the seaside took when they had business in the county court. It was the Rt. 13 of the 18th century.

In those days, Folly Creek was deeper and wider, and although you couldn't sail right up to the courthouse, you could sail to a landing not far away and get a wagon ride the rest of the way. During the 19th and 20th centuries, as farming techniques changed and land was tilled wide and deep, top soil was washed down to the creeks and once-navigable

waterways became impossible. Capt. Polk Lang once had an oyster packing house at the head of Folly Creek that employed 250 people during the winter season. Oyster House Road leads from Drummondtown Road down to the pilings where oyster monitors once tied up, and oysters were shucked and shipped across the country.

The northern margin of Joynes Neck is Parkers Creek, which also serves as the boundary for Baylys Neck, which adjoins Joynes, so to speak. Joynes and Baylys are not separated by a waterway, but each has its own access road, Rt. 652, Joynes Neck Road, and Rt. 662, Baylys Neck Road. Parkers Creek begins behind Metompkin Island and comes to an end near the old Mary N. Smith School on U.S. 13. Parker Creek Landing provides water access, and the Fox Grove residential community is adjacent to the landing. Accomac, nee Drummondtown, is the head of both necks.

I grew up fishing on Folly Creek and in my later years began exploring the upper waters, where siltation created a barrier for motor boats but offered a golden opportunity for those of us who often prefer a 13-foot Old Town Pack canoe to a fiberglass center console with dual Evinrudes and satellite navigation. Channel Point Farm is at the silted headwaters of Folly Creek, and I have spent many hours there either in boots or a small boat, watching great blue herons and wondering about the past. Centuries ago, this was part of an ancient highway, a marine corridor, an avenue of commerce, and once the site of an armed skirmish, where blood was shed to rid us from rule by a monarchy on the other side of the ocean.

Little is here now to speak of that. It is woods and farm fields, a few foundation stones from country club buildings prior to World War II, and of course the stream that quietly meanders from the residential communities of Accomac, through wooded glades and peaceful fields, finally becoming Folly Creek.

At Channel Point during the summer, when the woods are thick and the ticks are active, I explore in the Old Town Pack, a canoe made of Royalex weighing only 30 pounds or so. I can hoist it onto my shoulder, walk down to a convenient put-in, and be gone for the day.

Winter is the time for exploring Channel Point by foot, when the leaves have fallen and the forest is open, the bare branches of wild black cherry trees reaching for the sun like a basketball player going for a rebound. If the sun is out and the breeze is gentle, I will walk the farm fields. If it is blustery, I will seek shelter and let the run of the stream guide me through the woods. I always have my little recorder, a method of taking notes, my audible sketch pad that I can replay over and over.

I still have recorded notes from years ago of an encounter with a flock of cedar waxwings flitting between the cedars than line the farm road and a huge holly tree bejeweled with red berries. Beautiful birds, I noted, even though the day was heavily overcast and the subtle colors were not visible. The gray crest and stylish black mask gave the bird the look of a pirate from a 1940s operetta. They moved in unison in a flock of about twenty-five, fluttering down to drink in a puddle, then returning as one to the cedars or holly.

I once watched a red-tailed hawk hunting a fallow field that adjoined pine woods where the stream ran. I told my recorder that her primary feathers were spread like fingers, moving slightly to help balance her in flight. The hawk screamed as she hunted, a piercing cry that sounded like a small mammal in great distress. On a quiet day, the hawk's screech would carry for miles. My recorder got it.

If you want to experience the essence of an Eastern Shore neck, this is the place to be. The land is too wet for comfortable walking, and the water is too shallow to make way in a boat. This is where it begins.

Somewhere among the fallen trees and the tanglged vines of fox grape, a stream emerges from heavy, sodden soil, and it is joined by rivulets that slowly migrate down farm fields after a rain and come together under this shady canopy of sweet gums. Here is where Folly Creek begins. The hardwood swamp at Channel Point is the birthplace of Folly Creek, a community of springs and bogs, water that feels the pull of earth gravity in its birth, and will ultimately rise and fall in its maturity with the rhythm of moon gravity. If you want to taste the beginning of a neck, you are sucking on the marrow bone in here.

I have walked, paddled, or explored by skiff every foot of Folly Creek from its dark and private birthplace to the place where Folly Creek is set free. Like a fry that emerges from a fish egg, Folly Creek joins a vast school of waterways for a migration that will unite oceans.

In its infancy the creek is out of view, a stream that runs through woods and is buffered by soggy bottomland that both protects it and feeds it. The stream becomes the focus of Channel Point's animal and bird population. On both sides the leaves are matted and the ground packed by heavy traffic. An empty oyster shell is surrounded by raccoon prints. Deer drink along a sandy edge and leave their wedge-shaped foot prints in the damp earth. A titmouse bathes in the shallow water, shaking and fluffing its feathers.

From a distance the water appears rusty, but the rust actually is an orange algae growing on the bottom. Tiny filaments slow-dance in the current as the water leaves the farm and heads for the sea. Here and there along the stream are small, sandy beaches made of topsoil washed down with each heavy rain from an adjacent farm field. It is amazing how far topsoil can travel. The field is on the other side of the woods, at least a hundred yards away and still farther upstream. Yet down here in the woods, far removed, soil that once grew soybeans in the field has migrated to create a picnic beach for raccoons.

The little fans of topsoil are like growth rings in a tree. A band close to the field was washed down two years ago. One that empties into the creek proper is perhaps twenty-five years old; it left the field during a northeaster and is just now making the trip of several miles

Short-billed dowitchers at Cedar Island Station

to the deep part of the creek, and hence to the bay and the ocean.

The stream spirals around sweet gum roots, cutting away the soil and leaving a hard bank of gray clay and twisted wood. Strangely, the stream disappears underground, falling with a pleasant splash into an opening perhaps two feet in diameter covered with white foam. From there it runs underground – I can hear the flow of water – and emerges again some twenty feet away. A lush growth of moss covers the fallen trees and the exposed roots.

I make a misstep and go in over my boots, falling forward and grasping a small sassafras sappling. I pull myself out and realize that the tree in front of me is a deer rub, its bark worn away by a buck scraping the velvet from his rack.

Finally, the stream widens, though it is still shallow, and the vegetation changes. There now are cattails, marsh elders, the brown remnants of pickerelweed. Farther along, the spartina grasses begin to grow as the water becomes salty and widens to the size of a proper creek. *Spartina alterniflora*, a lush cordgrass, grows close to the water. In winter it is brown and lifeless, but in spring it will regain its vigor. Thick rhizomes embrace the muddy soil, holding it in a lacy grip. At the edge of the creek stands a great blue heron, a stern looking bird that paces the shallows like an impatient schoolmarm.

The water here is salty and tidal. The bottom is too soft to walk on -- a soupy mixture of decaying plant matter, topsoil from the farm field, fine sand weathered to powder. If I look at the mud with a magnifier, I would see the tiny grains, the bits of cellulose dropped by the rotting Spartina stems. Who knows what else is in there. Shellfish larvae, tiny plants called phytoplankton, bacteria, farm chemicals washed down with the topsoil – all these are part of the soup.

Around the bend of the creek I can see the derelict Coast Guard station on Cedar Island. From here the creek deepens, flows seaward with the pulse of tides. The woods ends and there is only salt marsh, and beyond that the inlet, where the water flows confidently, with dispatch. In the distance are sand dunes, low-slung tidal barriers cleaved by the inlet. And rising up beyond the dunes, white froth crisp against blue sky, is the Atlantic Ocean. The rhythmic surf has the sound of a beating heart. And I can feel the pulse.

Bowman's Folly and Cropper's Revenge

In February 1779, during the American Revolution, the British made a raid on Joynes Neck east of Drummondtown. It was more of a harassment than a skirmish, but in making the attack the British committed a grave tactical error. They pissed off John Cropper.

John Cropper lived on the north bank of Folly Creek on family land called Bowman's Folly, which he had inherited from Edmund Bowman. In 1776, as the war for Independence was beginning, Cropper was commissioned a captain in a Shore company of the 9th Virginia Regiment, which in December left to join George Washington in Morristown. In 1777 he was commissioned a major in the 7th Virginia Regiment and in September was wounded at the Battle of Brandywine. In 1778 General Lafayette appointed him lieutenant colonel in command of the 11th Virginia Regiment, and in June he participated in the Battle of Monmouth. In the fall he took a six-month furlough from the war and returned to Bowman's Folly to recuperate and spend time with his wife Margaret and their infant daughter, Sarah.

Cropper was 23 at the time and had been at war for three years, distinguishing himself not only as a tactician on the battlefield, but also as a leader of men. Before Cropper could leave for his next assignment, his life was changed by a contingent of British sailors aboard the ship tender *Thistle*, which accompanied a larger Navy vessel anchored offshore.

Late on a February night, just days before Cropper was to return to the 11th Virginia Regiment, a detachment from the British ship rowed through Metompkin Inlet, up Longboat Channel, and then headed

Bowman's Folly and Cropper's Revenge

west up Folly Creek. They approached Bowman's Folly with muffled oars and landed a short distance from the house where Cropper and his wife and baby were sleeping. The detachment surrounded the house, entered, and surprised Cropper and his family in their bed chamber. While the Croppers were held hostage, the attackers ransacked the house, pocketed the family jewelry, and destroyed the furniture.

The British troops discovered Cropper's stock of wine and liquors in the cellar, and soon the raid turned into a raucous party with most of the invaders quite drunk. Two men were guarding the bedroom where the family was being held, but as the guards became increasingly besotted, Cropper was able to slip away. He ran two miles in his skivvies to the house of the nearest neighbor, who also was engaged in the war, and the two of them loaded three muskets and returned to Cropper's home. Cropper and his neighbor neared the house and fired the three muskets in quick succession and began hollering loudly. "Let's go, boys. We've got them now!"

The British decided the party was over, and soon the tender they arrived in was heading seaward down Longboat Channel. Cropper freed Margaret and Sarah, who had been taken to an outbuilding, and as dawn came the Croppers made a grim discovery. A trail of gunpowder had been placed around the perimeter of the house, and if Cropper had not acted when he did, the house would have been destroyed.

No one was seriously injured in the attack, but the Cropper's home was wrecked, their furniture ruined, and their stock of wine, brandy, and single malt scotch exhausted. The event terrorized the young wife, and it intensified Cropper's hatred toward the British. Cropper was a young man, but he was a career soldier. As such, he abided by a certain code of ethics, and he expected others to do the same. To engage on the field of battle is one thing, but for soldiers to attack a private home and terrorize a family was unthinkable. The British had committed a serious transgression.

Were the British aware that the home was the residence of an officer in the American army? Or was it just a coincidence, young soldiers on a late-night raid of a civilian residence in search of food, drink, and other valuables? John Cropper was a young officer in the American army who made rank quickly. He was a star on the rise. Perhaps the British sought to diminish his glow.

In March Cropper was promoted again, receiving a commission of lieutenant colonel of the 7th Virginia Regiment, signed by John Jay, President of Congress. But Cropper was not comfortable leaving his young family alone again at Bowman's Folly. In August he resigned his commission, which the army refused to accept, yet he remained at home on an indefinite leave of absence.

Cropper had a vindictive streak, and although he was officially on leave of absence, he continued to harass the British at every opportunity. Ralph T. Whitelaw, writing in *Virginia's Eastern Shore*, relates an incident in which Cropper led a group of local militia in an attack on a British barge at Henry's Point, which is just down Folly Creek from Bowman's Folly, at a point where Folly Creek merges with Cross Creek.

Whitelaw says that the local militia attacked the crew of the barge as they were landing at Henry's Point, but the militia was driven back, leaving Cropper and a negro, George Latchom, actively engaged with the landing party. "The two kept up firing until the foe were within a few rods of them, when they were compelled to fall back," writes Whitelaw. "Cropper had to retreat through a sunken boggy marsh, in which he stuck fast up to his waist in soft mud, the enemy at the time being so close as to be about to bayonet him. At this critical juncture, the faithful colored man fired and killed the foremost man, seized hold of Cropper and dragged him by main strength out of the mud and taking him on his back carried him safely to dry land."

Latchom was a slave at the time, but was purchased and set free by Cropper, who befriended him in every way he could until Latchom's death.

Col. Cropper also participated in the Battle of the Barges in November 1782 in the Chesapeake Bay, the last naval battle of the Revolutionary War. Col. Cropper enlisted twenty-five local militia members to join Commodore Whaley of the Maryland Navy aboard his ship *Protector* in fighting Loyalist privateers at Kedges Strait near Tangier. The Maryland ship was badly out-gunned and after a fierce battle was forced to surrender. Twenty-six men died in the battle, including Commodore Whaley, who was buried with military honors in the cemetery at Scott Hall in Onancock. The colonel was badly wounded and taken prisoner, but was later released to return to Bowman's Folly to recuperate. The Battle of the Barges was Col. Cropper's last military action.

When the war was over, Cropper lived the life of a gentleman planter and politician. He served in the Virginia House of Delegates from 1784 to 1792. In 1793 he was commissioned lieutenant colonel of the 2nd Regiment of the Virginia Militia. When war with France was threatened in 1779, General Washington wrote Cropper and asked him to assume charge of raising troops from twenty-four Virginia counties. He served in the Virginia Senate from 1813 to 1817, and in 1815 he was commissioned Brigadier General with the 21st Brigade of Virginia Militia. General Cropper died on January 15, 1821 at age 66.

Over the years, several houses have stood on the Bowman's Folly site. The house Gen. Cropper lived in as a young man burned in 1815, and the showplace that is on the old plantation today was built shortly thereafter. Gen. Cropper had the property built up, and the home is on a mound a short distance back from Folly Creek, providing an unbroken view of the creek from the house site. From the creek, the old home provides a stately presence in the rural countryside.

The Croppers are one of a number of prominent families to have lived on the seaside of the Eastern Shore in the Accomac, or Drummondtown, area. These families provide an example of how closely knit the rural aristocracy was on the Eastern Shore. To the south were the Parramores of Bellevue Plantation, and to the north the Wises, Joyneses, Croppers, Baylys, and Bowmans. Gen. Cropper was married twice. His first wife, Margaret, was a Parramore. His second wife, Catherine, was a Bayly.

The general and Margaret had a daughter, Sarah, who survived the British invasion of her home in February, 1779. Sarah married John Wise, and their son, Henry A. Wise, became the first Virginia governor to have been born on the Eastern Shore.

Three Peninsulas at Attention

Three necks on the seaside vary from the notion that Eastern Shore necks are peninsulas in repose, that is, arranged at a right angle to the spine of the mainland. Between Wachapreague and Nassawadox lie Bradford Neck, Upshur Neck, and Bells Neck, all of which are roughly parallel to the spine. (Brickhouse Neck is similarly arranged but is an uninhabited marshy hummock and not accessible by county roads.)

Seaside necks were formed by a different geological phenomenon than those on the bayside, where the creeks drained the land and flowed into the Susquehanna River. On the seaside, the necks sometimes mimic the geology of the barrier islands, and the necks and the islands are parallel to each other. Indeed, at some point in geological time, the necks were likely barrier islands, and they might be once again in the future.

These three necks are the handiwork of the Machipongo River, the only Eastern Shore waterway deemed worthy of the designation "river." It flows for some twenty miles from Hog Island Bay, north of Fowling Point, all the way to Wachapreague. It is our longest tidal estuary, beginning at the expansive tidal flats along the county line where it is known as the Great Machipongo Channel. It flows northward from there, draining seaside communities and farmland via tributaries such as Red Bank Creek, Phillips Creek, Upshur Creek, and Greens Creek.

The Great Machipongo is deep and years ago was a major commercial thoroughfare, with schooners sailing from Red Bank Landing,

Brownsville, and Thomas Wharf to ports along the eastern United States and the Caribbean Islands. East of Exmore, at the waterfront village of Willis Wharf, the Machipongo divides, sending a fork called Parting Creek northward parallel to the main river, and thus creating Bells Neck, a low-slung ridge of marsh, farm fields, and pine woods. As the Machipongo River continues north, it defines the eastern boundary of Bells Neck and the western boundary of Upshur Neck, which faces Upshur Bay on its east side.

Parting Creek comes to an uncelebrated end east of Exmore, but the Machipongo meanders on, draining swampy enclaves with quizzical names such as Frog Stool and Piggen, creating little saltmarsh oxbows along the way. It flows under Piggen Road and divides itself into tidal creeks and drains and finally ditches that run all the way to Rt. 180, the Wachapreague Road.

In all its forms, and in all its nuances, the Great Machipongo River drainage is an exceptional landscape. The land it drains is rural, and the Machipongo is a wild place, and unless you go by boat, it is not easily observed. On Rt. 180 between Painter and Quinby the river can be seen at its best. The roadside view from the old crab packing shacks is panoramic. To the south is the northern end of Bells Neck, surrounded by thousands of acres of saltmarsh and tidal flats. North of the road the river begins its meandering run through the countryside, narrowing as it divides into watery tentacles that reach into the land. Enjoy the view with care. Rt. 180 is a busy secondary road.

Two other viewpoints are safer, if a bit off the beaten path. South of Rt. 180, Bells Neck Road intersects with Rt. 600 (Seaside Road) and provides access to Bells Neck. The road heads east, and then makes a sharp turn to the right. Here is an uninterrupted view of the crab shacks just mentioned about five miles to the north, and the village of Willis Wharf to the south. It is pure seaside landscape, an unbroken meadow of spartina grasses and saltwater bush for miles in both directions.

To see the upper reaches of the Machipongo, take Piggen Road (Rt. 622) to the point where it crosses the river. In a few miles, the river changes in character from a broad, strongly tidal waterway to freshets that drains forest and farmland.

Bradford Neck and Upshur Neck are arranged end to end, with the Machipongo River on the west flank. Bradford Neck is defined by Bradford Bay on the East, and Upshur Neck is defined by Upshur Bay. The two necks are divided, roughly, by the area of Quinby and the bridge that crosses the Machipongo there.

The head of Upshur Neck has historically been Warwick Plantation, just south of the Quinby community, where many generations of the Upshur family have lived since the 17th century. It is the family burying ground.

The community of Quinby is relatively new. It could easily be considered one of the railroad towns on the Eastern Shore in that prior to the railroad the area was known as Atlantic View Plantation, home of Littleton Thomas LeCato, who opened a store in the area, got a government contract to operate a post office, and in 1898 spearheaded the effort to build a bridge over the Machipongo River so local farmers could get their crops to the railroad in Painter. The bridge cut in half the distance farmers had to travel to reach the railroad when going to Keller.

The head of Bradford Neck is Wachapreague, which formerly was called Powellton, and prior to that Teackles Landing. Wachapreague, like Quinby, profited from the railroad, which provided an efficient way of getting plentiful local seafood to market. Wachapreague also became popular among sportsmen and tourists, and when A.G.H Mears opened the Hotel Wachapreague in 1902, the town became one of the most popular tourist destinations on the Virginia coast.

Tom LeCato's Bridge

Tom LeCato and Upshur Quinby were cousins and fast friends. Upshur lived at Warwick Plantation, the ancient family compound at the head of Upshur Neck. Tom lived at Atlantic View Plantation,

Quinby Bridge not long after construction
Courtesy of Carl H. Bundick

where his family settled on Bradford Neck at what now is Quinby. The boys grew up together and enjoyed fishing and hunting in the seaside marshes near their homes, and when they became adults they went their separate ways. Upshur went to law school at the University of Virginia and began a successful law practice, and Tom went to New York where he joined his father and brother in a produce brokerage business.

The boys did not see each other often, but the friendship endured over the years as they corresponded often and exchanged news about family and friends. Tom retired from the produce business around 1896, returned home to Bradford Neck, and he brought with him some of the entrepreneurial spirit that earned him success in the city. His granddaughter, Emma LeCato Eichelberger, wrote a biographical sketch about Tom in 1953, which was published in the *Peninsula Enterprise* newspaper of Accomac. "The years (in the city) had not accumulated money for him, but they had developed an inborn love of progress, a desire to see something done, something accomplished that would benefit the ordinary man. He was not long going to work (when he returned home)," she wrote.

Quinby was not a port town in those days. It was a farming area and local people who owned boats kept them tied up on private property at the head of a gut. The nearest store was five miles away. Mrs. Eichelberger wrote that Tom decided to open a store to serve the local community and to have a post office included with the store. He filled out the required forms, submitted them to the proper government agency, and the post office was approved, with the stipulation that Tom pick up the mail from the Keller post office three days a week and deliver it to his store to be distributed to the recipients. Tom agreed, and he was asked to provide a name for the post office. "Tom LeCato took great pleasure in naming the post office Quinby, for his boyhood friend," wrote Mrs. Eichelberger.

The railroad had opened on the Shore in 1884, providing a great marketing asset for local farmers, but Bradford Neck and Upshur Neck were miles from the nearest station. Most farmers continued to ship by boat because the nearest rail station was in Keller, some eight miles away. Tom LeCato realized that a direct line from Quinby to Painter would cut that distance in half, if a bridge could be built to span the Machipongo River.

Predictably, the plan met with opposition – "it can't be done, it will be too expensive" – but Tom believed that if he could convince people that a bridge would increase land values and provide more efficient marketing for farmers, it could be done. His brother, George W. LeCato, was in the Virginia Senate at the time and got a bill passed allowing a bridge with a draw to be built across the river, and a fundraising campaign was begun.

"Owners of neck land who lived elsewhere, and in some cases were people with money, saw it as a paying investment and took stock of $25 a share," wrote Mrs. Eichelberger. "Little by little the money came in until the needed amount, between two and three thousand dollars, was in hand."

The bridge builder was Francis Savage Smith, Tom LeCato's

brother-in-law, who managed to prove the nay-sayers wrong. He built a bridge that would carry traffic for more than thirty years, until the hurricane of 1933 wiped it out.

Machipongo Bridge opened for traffic on June 22, 1898. The span was 1,800-feet long, 16-feet wide, and came in at an on-budget cost of $2600. When the bridge was destroyed in 1933, the state highway department took it over and it re-opened on June 23, 1934.

The bridge transformed the little village that became Quinby. On twenty acres that once were part of Atlantic View Plantation were built homes, stores, a church, and dock facilities. A channel was cut by the government to provide access for watermen, and sport fishermen discovered the seaside community that separates Upshur Neck and Bradford Neck. Fisherman's Inn, a restaurant with vacation cabins, was built on the waterfront near the area where the harbor is today.

Bells Neck

Bells Neck, and its big sister, Upshur Neck, run north and south, parallel with the spine of the Eastern Shore, east of Painter and Exmore. Bells Neck is the western sister, lying close to the mainland. Parting Creek is on its west flank and the Machipongo River on the east. Upshur Neck is created by the Machipongo River and Upshur Bay and Hog Island Bay.

Historian Ralph T. Whitelaw wrote that Bells Neck was first patented in 1654 by Thomas Harmanson for 1,300 acres, but the neck changed hands numerous times during the seventeenth century, finally ending with a Bell ownership in 1697 when a Harmanson heir sold part of the neck to Robert Bell. Despite the Bell

ownership, the land was known as Nevilles Neck for much of the 18th century, and the creek separating the neck from the mainland was known as Nevilles Creek. The names Bells Neck and Parting Creek seem to have settled in during the early 20th century.

Bells Neck today is accessed by Bells Neck Road, which intersects with Seaside Road (Rt. 600) near the community of Coal Kiln. Years ago, according to Whitelaw, a horse bridge was located south of the current Bells Neck Road, near the area of the county line. Today there is only one way to reach Bells Neck, and that is via Bells Neck Road... unless you want to wade.

"There are a few houses in the neck which may have been built from the second quarter of the past century on, but none of them offer any special architectural features, or seem old enough to warrant detailed description," concluded Whitelaw. Whitelaw's dismissive attitude toward Bells Neck reflects his fascination with local architecture, but he misses an opportunity to point out a little-known jewel of the Eastern Shore landscape.

Bells Neck Road runs for three miles from Seaside Road along the shores of Parting Creek, coming to an end as it makes a sharp right turn and abruptly joins a soybean field at the southernmost extremity of Bells Neck. But the three-mile journey is one of the most pleasant on the Shore. The neck road runs east for about three-quarters of a mile, and then makes a sharp right turn. At this point, you can look to the north and see the Quinby Bridge and the old crab shedding shacks alongside it. Look to the south and you will see the village of Willis Wharf.

What we have here is an unobstructed view of several miles along a marshy avenue of grass that separates the mainland Eastern Shore from the islands. Farther south, with Hog Island and Cobbs Island some eight or ten miles from the mainland, this area is called the Broadwater because of the vast expanse of bays, tidal flats, and spartina marshes that lay between the islands and the upland. Here, it could be called the Broadmeadow. As the neck road crosses the marsh there are ditches and a few streams, but mostly there is spartina grass and

This is the view of Machipongo River from Rt. 180. The wooded area in the distance is the north end of Bells Neck.

black needlerush, and in fall, the jewel-like thickets of *Salicornia*, a succulent little plant oldtimers once used in salads.

Bells Neck Road parallels Parting Creek until the pavement ends among spent stems of soybeans. By the time it reaches the southern end of the neck, Parting Creek has become stretched thin. At low tide the creek is all mud flats and oyster rocks. When the tide begins to flood, the wading birds come in – herons and egrets – along with willets, yellowlegs, black-bellied plovers, and marbled godwits. In winter the waterfowl drop in to feed, the dabbling ducks up the creek guts and the little buffleheads diving in the channels.

Bells Neck exists in a kind of time warp, living on the edge. When scientists and planners discuss the effects of sea level rise, they need look no farther than this neck of land, such a pleasant and gentle landscape, but one that is changing. Low lying fields that once grew sweet potatoes now grow saltmeadow hay. People still live in Bells Neck, and the high land is farmed. Ironically, the highest land is on the southern end of the neck, just across Parting Creek from Willis Wharf. It is along the northern portion of Bells Neck Road where the high tides encroach. And so, we have an enigma. There will be a Bells Neck for many more generations. But how will we get there?

Coda

"We thought sea level rise was a creeping phenomenon, nobody knew it would be a galloping beast."

– Rod Hennessey

In the late 1970s Rod Hennessey bought 120 acres of land in Bells Neck. It was a combination of farm land, pine forest, and saltmarsh, a wild slice of the seaside that was part of the landscape Rod had been hired to protect. Rod had recently joined The Nature Conservancy as the first manager of the Virginia Coast Reserve, which today consists of more than 30,000 acres of barrier islands, saltmarsh, and contiguous mainland stretching from Smith Island northward to Wallops.

Rod is a native of New Jersey, a graduate of Rutgers University and the Yale School of Forestry, and he knew all about the effects intensive development could bring to coastal ecosystems. New Jersey had precious few of its coastal landscapes left intact. On the Virginia coast, Rod had an opportunity to protect an ecosystem that was in its original condition. The islands once had villages and gunning clubs, but these were part of the history of the landscape. Rod's mission was to protect one of the few remaining intact barrier island systems on the entire coast. His 120-acre Bells Neck farm would be part of it.

Rod was 25 and single at the time, and in a forested section of his farm he built a small house that provided a sweeping view of the

Machipongo River to the east and Parting Creek to the west. A great meadow of spartina spread like a saltmarsh prairie between Rod's pine woods and the river. For a recent graduate of the Yale School of Forestry, it was the perfect bachelor pad.

The bachelor pad was short-lived. Rod met a local girl, a schoolteacher named Martha West, and the two of them hit it off. They married, the bachelor pad got a sizeable addition, and Martha moved in, becoming one of the few residents of remote Bells Neck. "My mother wasn't happy about it," she says. "I was teaching at Broadwater Academy and had a house nearby in Exmore, and she thought Bells Neck was too remote. She lived in Birdsnest and she thought that was remote. I told her I loved it down there in the neck. It was a beautiful landscape, peaceful and quiet."

The Hennesseys raised two sons in Bells Neck. Patrick is an officer in the Coast Guard and Connor teaches at Broadwater, and the two boys enjoyed growing up hunting and fishing and enjoying the rural lifestyle. Would they one day have families and return to the farm where they grew up?

Unfortunately, the answer to that question has likely been made for them, by Mother Nature. The sea level is rising, and Bells Neck is sinking. In just a few years, farmland has become wetland and the forests are dying because of salt water inundation. The necks of the Eastern Shore, the first places chosen as homes when the English settled here, are becoming unlivable. Some have high land, but most are at or near sea level. The tidal creeks are growing wider, and the necks are becoming narrower. And it is happening quickly.

"Nobody anticipated it to happen like this," says Rod. "We thought sea level was a creeping phenomenon, nobody knew it was going to be a galloping beast."

Bells Neck is taking a beating from the galloping beast now, but the beast will likely make itself known among other necks that, like Bells Neck, are low in elevation. "It's always in the back of my mind," says Rod. "It's not bad to be flooded in, but it's not good to be flooded out." Tidal charts are frequently consulted when planning outings.

"The frustrating thing, when the boys were in school, was going out to a basketball game at night and coming home at eleven o'clock and finding the road flooded. We would have to turn around and go spend the night with my mother," says Martha.

In just a few years, the changes in the landscape have been remarkable. "I have been watching a spot out there in the marsh that started as a mud bog the size of a bathtub a few years ago, and now it is covered with tidal water and it attracts shorebirds and ducks in the winter," says Rod. "The marsh is becoming mud flats and the pine woods are becoming ghost forests. The trees are dying."

A few years ago, the state highway department built up the road, but it still floods during high tides. Only one road provides access to the neck, and a vulnerable low spot is near where the road enters the neck on the north end. The highest land in the neck is on the south end, meaning that access is limited for residents, even though their property may not be under water.

Only four families are full time residents of Bells Neck, and county and state agencies are facing a dilemma in justifying the cost of providing services such as road maintenance and utilities. The neck still has some productive farm land, but is it fair for taxpayers to foot the bill for expensive road upgrades to provide access to a limited resource?

Rod was once a proponent of engineered solutions such as dikes and flood gates, but he knows that is unlikely to happen in Bells Neck. "Nobody is in favor of dikes. The concept now is passive, and the current phrase is resilience. Let it become natural. We could move the house two hundred yards to a higher spot and get maybe another hundred years, but the weak point is the road on the north end of the neck."

The rising sea has created an evolution within the landscape. The creeks are wide. The necks are narrow. Someday soon, the neck will become an island. And the peninsula will be a demi-isle no more.

Glossary

Eastern Shore Necks, the Waters that Create Them, and the Heads of the Necks (HON), where applicable:

NORTHAMPTON COUNTY

Bayside Necks, from the south:

- Old Plantation: Old Plantation and Kings Creek
- Eyre Hall: Eyre Hall, Eyreville, and Cherrystone Creeks
- Eyreville: Eyreville and Old Castle Creeks
- Savage: The Gulf, Chesapeake Bay, Cherrystone Inlet, Old Castle Creek, HON: Eastville
- Old Town: Mattawoman Creek and The Gulf, HON: Eastville
- Wilsonia: Hungars and Mattawoman Creeks, HON: Shadyside
- Church: Church Creek and Hungars Creek, HON: Bridgetown
- Elliotts: Warehouse and Church Creeks, Port: Bayford
- Wellington: Holly Grove and Warehouse Creeks, HON Franktown

Seaside necks, from the south:

- Indiantown: Indiantown Creek and Taylor Creek, HON: Eastville
- Holt Neck: Indiantown Creek and Ramshorn Channel
- Brickhouse: Castle Ridge Creek and Red Bank Creek

ACCOMACK COUNTY

Bayside, from the south:

- Scarburgh: Craddock and Occohannock Creeks, HON: Belle Haven
- Craddock: Nandua and Craddock Creeks, HON: Craddockville
- Island Neck: Currituck Creek and McLean Gut
- Fairview: Boggs Gut, Nandua Creek, and McLean Gut
- Hacks: Pungoteague and Nandua Creeks, Chesapeake Bay, HON: Pungoteague, Port: Harborton
- Yeo: Pungoteague and Taylor Creeks, HON: Bobtown
- Red Bank: Warehouse Prong and Bull Branch of Pungoteague Creek, HON: Little Hell
- Sluitkill: Matchotank and Underhill Creeks, HON: Cashville
- Broadway: Parkers and Matchotank Creeks, HON: Cashville
- Finneys: Parkers and Finneys Creeks, HON: Onancock
- Baileys: Finneys and Onancock Creeks, HON: Onancock
- Coe's Out: Muddy Creek and Guilford Creek, HON: Guilford
- Pocomoke: Holden and Messongo Creeks
- Jollys: Bullbeggar and Holden Creeks

Seaside, from the south:

- Upshur: Machipongo River, Upshur Bay, Hog Island Bay, HON: Warwick Plantation
- Bells: Machipongo River, Parting Creek, HON: Cats Bridge
- Bradford: Machipongo River, Bradford Bay, HON: Wachapreague
- Custis: Custis and Folly Creeks, HON: Daugherty

- Joynes: Folly and Parkers Creeks, HON: Accomac
- Baylys: Folly and Parkers Creeks, HON: Accomac
- Parkers: Bundick and Parkers Creeks
- Whites: Bundick and Crippen Creeks and Whites Creek and Mutton Hunk Branch
- Gargathy: Mutton Hunk Branch, Gargathy Creek
- Hog: Gargathy Creek, Kegotank Bay, Hog Neck Creek
- Arbuckle: Assawoman Creek and Hog Creek
- Wallops: Mosquito Creek and Simoneaston Bay, HON: Wattsville
- Winders: Swans Gut Creek, Coldkill Creek, and Chincoteague Bay, HON: Horntown

Bibliography

Ames, Susie M.
The Company's Garden: Dale's Gift
Hickory House, 1998

Ames, Susie M.
Studies of the Virginia Eastern Shore in the Seventeenth Century
The Dietz Press, 1940

Ames, Susie M.
County Court Records of Accomack-Northampton, Virginia, 1640-1645
Virginia Historical Society, 1973

Badger, Curtis J.
Bellevue Farm – Exploring Virginia's Coastal Countryside
Stackpole Books, 1997

Badger, Curtis J.
"Guy Taplin – A British Carver with an American Vision"
Wildfowl and Collecting, Spring 1991, page 41

Badger, Curtis J. and Lynn M.
Letters Home – Of Gold Fields and Lost Ships
Salt Water Media, 2014

BIBLIOGRAPHY

Badger, Curtis J.
Salt Tide – Cycles and Currents of Life Along the Coast
Countryman Press, 1999

Badger, Curtis J.
Wilderness Regained - The Story of the Virginia Barrier Islands
Salt Water Media, 2022

Barnes, Brooks Miles and William G. Thomas
The Countryside Transformed: The Railroad and the Eastern Shore of Virginia, 1870-1935. A Collaborative Effort of the Eastern Shore of Virginia Public Library and the Virginia Center for Digital History of the University of Virginia, 2008.

Brown, Alexander Crosby
Steam Packets on the Chesapeake – A History of the Old Bay Line since 1840
Cornell Maritime Press, 1961

Doughty, L.E.
A Narrative About Life on Hog Island, Va.
Hickory House, 2002

Egloff, Keith and Deborah Woodward
First People – The Early Indians of Virginia
Virginia Department of Historic Resources, 1992

Farlow, Jackie M.
High Tide in Jackie's Kitchen
Privately published, 1990

Fitzhugh, Georgiana
The Life of Dr. John Tankard
Hampton Institute Press, 1907

Hall, Jenean
An "Uncertain Rumor" of Land – New Thoughts on the English Founding of Virginia's Eastern Shore
KWE Publishing, 2022

Hunter, Alexander
Huntsman in the South
Neale Publishing Company, 1908

Kacirk, Jeffrey
The Word Museum – The Most Remarkable English Words Ever Forgotten
Touchstone, 2000

Kester-McCabe, Dana
The Persistent Buccaneer
Moonshell Productions, 2020

Kolp, John G.
"'Mrs. Ann' and 'The Colonel' -- The Limits of Gendered Power on the Eastern Shore of Virginia"
Virginia Magazine of History and Biography, Vol. 130 No. 3, pages 218-252
Virginia Historical Society, 2022

Kurlansky, Mark
Salt – A World History
Penguin, 2002

LeCato, Nathaniel J.W.
Tom Burton Or the Days of 1861
Out-of-print, publisher unknown, 1888

Loundsbury, Carl R., Ed.
The Material World of Eyre Hall
Maryland Center for History and Culture, 2021

Mason, A Hughlett
History of Steam Navigation to the Eastern Shore of Virginia
Dietz Press, 1973

Mears, James Egbert
Hacks Neck and Its People, Past and Present
Privately published, 1937

Mears, James Egbert
The Eastern Shore During the War of Secession Period and Reconstruction
Unpublished bound manuscript

Mears, James Egbert
The Eastern Shore – Maryland and Virginia
Charles B. Clark, ed.
Lewis Historical, 1950

Miles, M.K.
MilesFiles, An online genealogical database
Eastern Shore of Virginia Heritage Center (ESPL)
Updated on a regular basis

Perry, James R.
The Formation of a Society on Virginia's Eastern Shore, 1615-1655
University of North Carolina Press, 1990

Proulx, Annie
The Shipping News
Scribners, 1993

Rountree, Helen C. and Thomas E. Davidson
Eastern Shore Indians of Virginia and Maryland
University of Virginia Press, 1997

Shiras, George 3d
Hunting Wild Life with Camera and Flashlight
National Geographic Society, 1935

Upshur, John Andrews
Upshur Family in Virginia
2nd Edition by Robert Irving Upshur and Thomas Teakle Upshur IV
Warwick House Publishing, 1993, originally published 1953

Whitelaw, Ralph T.
Virginia's Eastern Shore – A History of Northampton and Accomack Counties
Peter Smith edition, 1968
Virginia Historical Society, 1951

Wise, Jennings C.
Ye Kingdome of Accawmacke or the Eastern Shore of Virginia in the Seventeenth Century
The Bell Book and Stationary Co., 1911

Wise, John Sergeant
The End of an Era
Houghton, Mifflin and Company, 1899

Index

A

Accawmacke 21
Accomac iv, 8, 33, 47, 48, 49, 66, 83, 101, 103, 111, 121, 127, 138, 139, 140, 147, 151, 161
Accomack County iv, v, 3, 6, 8, 23, 25, 31, 34, 36, 40, 55, 57, 58, 63, 73, 75, 88, 96, 98, 104, 107, 120, 121, 160
Addison, John 90
Aeschliman, Bill 105
Agricultural Experiment Station 9
American Fish Guano Company 124, 125
American Revolutionary War 24, 33, 47, 95, 115, 121, 144, 146
Ames, Susie May i, 31, 33, 55, 57, 58, 59, 63, 73, 76, 128
Ames, Tank 92
Anchor 122
Annamessex Creek 22
Annapolis, Maryland 43
An *"Uncertaine Rumor" of Land – New Thoughts on the English Founding of Virginia's Eastern Shore* 18
Arbuckle Neck vii, 8, 65, iv
Arbuckle Neck Road 2
Arcadia 23
Arlington, Virginia 25, 29
Arnold, Jim (Captain) 93
Ashby, Abel Thomas 98
Ashby, Ben 98
Ashby, Jimmie 98
Ashby, Samuel 99
Ashby, Thomas 89, 99
Assateague Island 24, 75, 90, 124
Assateague Island National Seashore 135
Assawoman vii, 22, 24, 65
Assawoman Creek 8, 161
Atlantic 25, 56
Atlantic City, New Jersey 108
Atlantic Hotel 28
Atlantic Ocean iv, v, vi, vii, 1, 29, 52, 59, 73, 143
Atlantic View Plantation 150, 153
Audubon 137

B

Badger, John (Captain) 60, 61, 62, 63, 66, 79
Badger, Lynn ii, 103
Badger, Thomas 60, 61, 66
Badger, Tom 103
Baileys Neck 8, iv
Baldwin family 13, 14

Baldwin, Furlong 14
Baltimore, Maryland 14, 66, 79, 81, 82, 83, 85, 86, 92, 93, 106, 123
Baltimore Steam Packet Company 80. See also Old Bay Line
Baltimore Sun 82
Barnes, Brooks Miles i, 4, 24, 58, 78, 128
Bassett Hall 44
Battle of the Barges 146, 147
Battle Point 91, 94, 95
Bayford 159
Baylys Neck 8, 139, iv
Baylys Neck Road 139
bayside v, vii, 1, 2, 3, 4, 5, 6, 7, 8, 9, 13, 20, 22, 23, 36, 64, 72, 83, 85, 90, 95, 104, 113, 119, 124, 127, 148, 159, 160
Bayside Road 25
Belle Haven iv, v, 10, 24, 25, 91, 104, 106, 107, 127, 128, 160
Bellevue Plantation 33, 147
Bell, Robert 153
Bells Neck i, 3, 148, 149, 153, 154, 155, 156, 157, 158, iv
Bells Neck Road 149, 154, 155
Bennett, Covington (Covy) Sr. 120
Bennett, Elizabeth Mears 120
Bennett, James "Jim" H. 113, 115, 116, 117, 120, 121, 126
Bennett, John 113
Bennett, Margaret (Peggy) Caruthers 120
Bennett, Margaret Watson 120
Bennett, Rachel Shrieves 120
Bennett, Teakle 113
Bennett, Thomas Henry 126
Bennett, William (Captain) 115, 120

Bermuda 121
Bethel Methodist Church 89, 90
Beth Haven 24. See also Belle Haven
Big Pine Road 118, 129
Birdsnest iii, 157
blockade 61, 114, 115, 118, 119, 120, 121
blockade runners i, 113, 115, 117, 118, 120, 121, 126
blockade running 114, 117, 118, 119, 120
Blore, Frances 18
Blore, John 18
Blower, John 33
Bloxom iv
Bobtown 128, 160
Boggs, Frank (Captain) 84
Boggs, George i, 107, 108
Boggs Gut 160
Boggs, Levi 121
Boggs, Mattie Sarah 108
Boggs, Myra 83, 84, 85, 86
Boggs Wharf 80, 84, 128
Boggs Wharf Road 20
Bona Venture 33
Bowman's Folly 144, 145, 146, 147
Bradford Bay 150, 160
Bradford Neck vii, 3, 148, 150, 151, 152, 153, iv
Brickhouse Neck 148, 159
bridge 64, 79, 86, 150, 152, 153, 154
Bridgetown v, vii, 24, 25, 39, 64, 91, 127, 159
Broadmeadow 154
Broadwater 4, 6, 154
Broadwater Academy 157
Broadway Neck 8, iv
Brokaw, William B. (Captain) 113
Brownsville 36, 43, 95, 149

INDEX

Brownsville Plantation 39, 48
Buckland Gut 118
Bullbeggar Creek 60, 160
Bull Branch 160
Bull Farm 43
Bull Run vii, 65. See also Daugherty
Bundick, Carl H. 151
Bundick Creek 161
Butcher Creek 115, 118, 126

C

Camden, Nancy Byrd 105, 106
Campbell, Gordon i, viii
Cape Charles iii, vi, 6, 11, 96
Cape Charles City iii, 11, 25, 26
Cape Henry iii
Cape May 86
Capeville 25
Caserta 43
Cashville 5, 84, 160
Castle Ridge Creek 159
Cats Bridge 160
Cattail Neck 8
Cedar Grove 36, 39
Cedar Island 24, 124, 138, 142, 143
Cedar Island Station 142
Cedar View 128
Chair Place 105
Channel Point Farm 138, 139, 140, 141
Cheriton iii, vi
Cherrystone Creek 13, 22, 86, 159
Cherrystone Inlet vi, 13, 17, 159
Cherrystone Wharf 25, 57, 104, 127
Chesapeake Bay iii, iv, vi, vii, 1, 4, 10, 15, 28, 29, 50, 63, 72, 74, 76, 81, 82, 88, 94, 104, 114, 118, 119, 124, 131, 133, 146, 159, 160
Chesapeake Bay Bridge 79, 80
Chesapeake Bay Bridge-Tunnel 14, 79, 96
Chesconnessex Creek 22, 71
Chincoteague Bay 3, 161
Chincoteague Island iv, 22, 23, 24, 25, 27, 28, 51, 65, 75, 124
Church Creek 4, 159
Church Neck iii, vi, vii, 4, 36, 40, 44, 64, 69, 101, 159
Civil War 19, 25, 31, 32, 52, 61, 63, 83, 84, 91, 92, 95, 97, 113, 117, 127
Coal Kiln 154
Cobb family 25, 52, 53
Cobb, Nathan Jr. 52, 53
Cobbs Island 25, 51, 53, 154
Coe's Out Neck 8, iv
Coe, Timothy 8
Coldkill Creek 3, 161
Colonna, John 98
Colonna, Trissie 105, 106
Concord Wharf 10, 25, 90, 91, 92, 93
Confederacy 115, 118, 121
Confederate 114, 121
Craddock 102, 103, 110
Craddock and Occohannock Academy 107
Craddock Creek 9, 102, 104, 109, 160
Craddock Neck i, 9, 66, 81, 101, 102, 103, 104, 105, 107, 109, iv
Craddock Neck Road 104
Craddockville v, 9, 90, 102, 104, 105, 108, 128, 160
Craddockville Road 108
Crippen Creek 161
Crisfield, Maryland 86
Cropper, Catherine Bayly 147

169

Cropper family 147
Cropper, John (General) 144, 145, 146, 147
Cropper, Margaret Parramore 144, 145, 147
Cropper, Sarah 144, 145, 147
Cross Creek 146
Crossroads vii. See also Onley
Currituck 102, 110
Currituck Creek 104, 160
Custis Creek 160
Custis, John 37
Custis Neck vii, 8, 65, iv
Custis Pond 17, 135

D

Dale's Gift 14, 15, 54
Dale, Thomas 54
Darby, William 130
Daugherty vii, 65, 160
Davis Wharf 9, 20, 25, 128
Davis Wharf Road 20
Debdeavon 17, 18
Declaration of Independence 38, 58, 71
Delaware Bay 29
Deliverance 121
Delmarva 86
Delmarva Peninsula 1, 28, 80, 88
demi-isle ii, 1, 3, 158
Dixon, Rev. Thomas 26
Dolly Varden 95
Drewer, John 107
Drummond, Ellis 109
Drummond, Harry W. 107
Drummondtown 8, 23, 25, 91, 115, 120, 127, 138, 139, 144

Drummondtown Road 139
Drummond, Walter 107
Dunton family 46

E

Easley, Mary 111
Eastern Shore 84, 85, 86, 94
Eastern Shore of Virginia Heritage Center (ESPL) 32, 88, 120, 127
Eastern Shore of Virginia National Wildlife Refuge 14
Eastern Shore of Virginia Produce Exchange 123
Eastern Shore Railroad 25
Eastern Shore Steamboat Company 81, 83, 85, 86, 93, 94
Eastern Shore Yacht and Country Club viii, 9
Eastville iii, vi, 17, 24, 25, 29, 43, 89, 91, 115, 117, 127, 131, 135, 159
Eastville Inn 17, 29
education 70, 96, 98, 99, 100
Eichelberger, Emma LeCato 151, 152
Elliotts Neck vi, 4, 159
Elliott, Thomas G. 66
Emily Agnes 123
Ennis, Joseph 99
Essex 39. See also Point Farm
Essex County, England 34, 35, 37, 49, 50, 51
Evans Wharf 80, 84
Evans Wharf Road 20
Exmore iii, vi, 10, 92, 96, 106, 149, 153, 157
Exmore-Willis Wharf High School 99
Eyre, Benjamin 31

Eyre family 13, 14
Eyre Hall 13, 14
Eyre Hall Creek 13, 159
Eyre Hall Neck vi, 3, 159
Eyre, John 41
Eyre, Littleton 13
Eyre, Martha 31
Eyre, Reginald 31
Eyreville Creek 13, 159
Eyreville Neck vi, 3, 13, 17, 159

F

Fair Oaks 65
Fairview Neck 9, iv
Farlow, Charlie 102, 103
Farlow, Jackie 102, 103, 111
fertilizer 82, 123
Finneys Creek 8, 36, 46, 65, 160
Finneys Island 8
Finneys Neck 8, iv
Finneys Wharf 81
Finneys Wharf Road 20
Fisherman Island vi, 15
Fisherman's Inn 153
Folly Creek 8, 138, 139, 140, 141, 144, 145, 146, 147, 160, 161
Forest and Stream 66
Fowling Point 148
Fowlkes Tavern 129, 130
Fox Grove 139
Franklin City 27, 28
Franktown v, 4, 23, 25, 43, 64, 91, 99, 104, 127, 159
Franktown High School 97
Franktown-Nassawadox High School 88, 99, 100
Freeschool Neck 8. See also Pocomoke Neck
Frog Stool 149

G

Gargaphia Plantation 8, 69, 70, 71, 72, 74, 75, 77
Gargatha 69
Gargatha Inlet 24
Gargathy Creek 8, 69, 161
Gargathy Neck i, 8, 38, 55, 58, 69, 70, 72, 74, 90, 110, iv
Gloucester County 36, 70, 113
gold 60, 61, 87
goose 59
goosery 59
Great Machipongo Channel 148
Great Machipongo River 149
Great Neck 4
Greens Creek 148
guano 123, 124, 126
Guilford 8, 25, 127, 160
Guilford Creek 8, 57, 160
Guilford Wharf 65
Gwynn's Island 113

H

Hack, George (Doctor) 9, 127
Hacks Neck i, viii, 9, 31, 65, 104, 113, 115, 117, 118, 120, 121, 124, 126, 127, 128, 129, 130, iv
Hacks Neck and Its People, Past and Present 9, 31, 117, 127
Hacks Neck Navy 115
Hadlock v, 25, 91, 104, 127
Hall, Jenean i, 18
hammock 7, 8. See also hummock

Hamp 91
Hampton 80
Hancock Gut 118
Hannah A. Lennon 125
Harborton viii, 25, 65, 80, 82, 124, 125, 126, 128, 160. See also Hoffman's Wharf
Harborton Road 129
Harlan and Hollingsworth 30, 83, 84
Harmanson, Thomas 153
Harper's New Monthly Magazine 28
Harrison, Fred (Captain) 111
Hawk's Nest 65
Heath, Milton 99
Hedra Cottage 72, 75
Helen 84, 86, 92, 93, 94
Hennessey, Connor 157
Hennessey, Martha West i, 157, 158
Hennessey, Patrick 157
Hennessey, Rod i, 156, 157, 158
Henry's Point 146
High Tide in Jackie's Kitchen 111
History of Steam Navigation to the Eastern Shore of Virginia 86
Hoffmans 126
Hoffman's Wharf 25, 65, 80, 123, 124, 125, 126
Hog Creek 8, 161
Hog Island 8, 23, 24, 29, 102, 103, 154
Hog Island Bay vi, 3, 39, 148, 153, 160
Hog Neck 8, iv
Hog Neck Creek 8, 161
hogshead 122
Holden Creek 8, 60, 160
Holly Grove Creek 159
Holt Neck vi, 159
Homann, Johann Baptist 23
Hornsby, Anah 107

Hornsby, James 107
Horntown vii, 23, 25, 161
Horse Hole Creek 118
Hotel Wachapreague 150
Howard, Philip 130
hummock 8, 148
Hungars 57
Hungars Church 39
Hungars Creek iii, vi, vii, 4, 11, 22, 37, 40, 64, 86, 159
Hunter, Alexander 25, 26
Hunting Creek 65
Hunting Wild Life With Camera and Flashlight 26, 27
Huntsman in the South 26
H.W. Drummond, Inc. 107
Hygiea 80
Hyslop Marsh 104

I

incognita land 27
indenture 31, 32, 33, 35, 36, 37, 38, 50, 63, 70, 71, 77, 121
Indiantown Creek 159
Indiantown Neck vi, 159
Island Neck 9, iv

J

Jacobus Creek 4
James City 14, 15, 18, 50, 56, 74, 75
James, Hez 98
James, H.P. Jr. 91
James L. Day 60
James River 86
Jamestown 18, 54, 55, 57, 74, 90
Jamesville 10, 54, 89, 90, 91, 92, 98,

99
James Wharf 92
Janie 95
Jenifer, Daniel 38, 58, 70, 71, 75, 76
Jenifer, Daniel Jr. (of St. Thomas) 75, 76
John and Francis 18
Johnson, Clinton 107
Johnson, Thomas 89, 93
Johnsontown vi, 91
Jollys Neck 8, 60, iv
Joynes Neck i, 8, 137, 138, 139, 144, iv
Joynes Neck Road 139
Joynes, Tully 94
J. W. 123
J.W. Hawkins 125

K

Kedges Strait 146
Kegotank Bay 161
Kellam, Omar 112
Keller iii, iv, 126, 128, 150, 152
Killmon, John Jr. 107
Kimble, Sammy 116
Kings Creek iii, 3, 24, 57, 159
Kiptopeke 86
Kolp, John G. 73, 74, 75

L

Lang, Polk (Captain) 139
Latchom, George 146
Laws, Martin 115, 116
LeCato, George W. 152
LeCato, Littleton Thomas 150
LeCato, Nathaniel J.W. 120
LeCato, Tom 150, 151, 152

Little Creek 86
Little Hattie 122
Little Hell 160
Little Machipongo Inlet 24
Little Mosquito Creek 4
Locust Mount 25
Locustville vii, 25
Longboat Channel 144, 145
Louisiana 61, 62
Lower Rack Island 24

M

Machipongo vi, 149
Machipongo Bridge 153
Machipongo Inlet Coast Guard Station 102
Machipongo River 3, 39, 148, 149, 150, 152, 153, 155, 157, 160
Magothy Bay 13, 72
Mapp, A.N.H. 91, 92
Mapp, Ed 98
Mapp, Harry 99
Mappsburg 65, 128
Mariner, Kirk 130
Marionville 25
Martin, John 130
Martin's Wharf 104
Maryland Center for History and Culture 14
Mary N. Smith School 139
Mason, A. Hughlett 82, 83, 86
Matchotank Creek 160
Mathews 113
Mattawoman Creek 4, 37, 159
Matthapunko Island 23
Matthews, Alton 56
McLean Gut 160

173

McMaster Old Home Essay 88
McMath, George 101
Mears, A.G.H. 150
Mears, James E. i, 6, 9, 31, 117, 119, 120, 124, 125, 126, 127, 128, 129
Mears' Wharf 81. See also Poplar Cove
Melfa iv, 65
Melson, Bobbie 112
Melson, Jack (Captain) 66, 102, 111
Melson Methodist Church 93
menhaden 124, 125, 126
Menhaden Fish and Oil Company 125. See also American Fish Guano Company
Merlin 137, 138
Merrimac 122
Messongo Creek 8, 160
Messongo Neck 8
Metompkin 25
Metompkin Inlet 138, 144
Metompkin Island 24, 69, 138, 139
Metompkin Road 70
MilesFiles 32, 120, 126
Miles, Kim i
Miles, M.K. i
Mill Branch 89
Minho 122
Mitchell, Samuel A. 25
Mobjack Bay 113
Mockhorn Island 54
Modest Town 25
Moore, Martin 74, 77
Morgan, Arnold 121
Morley family 93
Morley's Wharf 9, 10, 20, 88, 92
Morley's Wharf Road 20
Morse, Albro J. 125, 126

Morse family 126
Mosquito Creek 4, 161
Mount Airy 90
Mt. Nebo 84
Muddy Creek 8, 160
Mutton Hunk 69
Mutton Hunk Branch 69, 161
Myrtle Island 250

N

Nabb Center 88
Nandua 79, 83, 84, 86, 128
Nandua Creek 9, 22, 102, 104, 117, 126, 160
NASA. See also Wallops Flight Facility
Nassawadox iii, vi, vii, 36, 97, 99, 148
Nassawadox Creek vi, 4, 6, 10, 54, 57, 88, 90, 91, 92, 93, 94
National Geographic Magazine 26, 27
National Geographic Society 26
Nelson, Bill i, iv, vi
Nelsonia iv
Nevilles Creek 154
Nevilles Neck 154
New Church iv
Newport, Christopher 18, 19
Newtown 113
New York City 26, 28
New York, Philadelphia and Norfolk Railroad 6, 11, 25, 95
Norfolk Landmark 11
Norfolk, Virginia 43, 82, 123
Northampton-Accomack Memorial Hospital 49
Northampton County v, vi, vii, 3, 6, 9, 11, 13, 20, 23, 25, 34, 37, 38, 39,

40, 41, 42, 48, 57, 72, 83, 88, 96, 98, 99, 104, 159
Northampton County School Board 99
Nottingham family 46
Nussawattox iii, vii

O

Oak Hall iv
Occohannock Creek vi, 9, 10, 11, 20, 22, 38, 39, 50, 72, 75, 88, 92, 93, 94, 160
Occohannock Neck vi, 4, 9, 10, 36, 38, 39, 54, 69, 88, 89, 90, 92, 94, 95, 99, 100, 101
Ochiawampe 89
Off 13 130
Old Bay Line 80, 82
Old Castle Creek 17, 159
Old Plantation iii, 13, 14, 15
Old Plantation Creek vi, 3, 11, 22, 65, 159
Old Plantation Neck 3, 159
Old Town Neck vi, 4, 17, 43, 159
Onancock iv, vii, 23, 94, 124, 127, 147, 160
Onancock Creek iv, 8, 9, 22, 81, 101, 160
Onley iv, vii, 96
ordinary iii, v, 64, 65, 66, 72, 77
Oyster House Road 139
oysters 28, 50, 81, 92, 93, 102, 109, 110, 118, 139, 141, 155

P

Painter iii, iv, 9, 128, 149, 150, 152, 153

Panama 61, 62, 79
Parker, Jo Sue Drummond 105, 106, 107
Parker Neck iv
Parkers Creek 139, 160, 161
Parkers Creek Landing 139
Parker, Severn E. (General) 41
Parkers Marsh 8
Parkers Neck 8, 161
Parks, Benjamin iv
Parksley iv, 88, 96, 127
Parramore family 33, 147
Parramore Island 23
Parramore, John 33
Parramore, Thomas C. (Judge) 65
Parting Creek 3, 149, 153, 154, 155, 157, 160
Peninsula Enterprise 10, 59, 60, 83, 121, 151
Peninsula Telephone Company 126
Pennsylvania Railroad 25
Pennyville 128
Phebe 122
Philadelphia, Pennsylvania 25, 59, 93, 108
Philibosian, Scarlett ii
Phillips Creek 148
Piggen 149
Piggen Road 149
Pitt, Robert 63
Pitts Creek 57
Pitts Neck 8, iv
Pitts Wharf 25
Plantation Creek 57
Pleiades 122
Pocahontas 17, 18
Pocomoke Creek 22
Pocomoke Neck 8, iv

Pocomoke River iv, 63, 83
Point Farm 39. See also Essex
Pope family 40
Poplar Cove 81
Pork Chop Hill 108
potatoes 11, 56, 62, 64, 81, 84, 86, 102
Potomac River 38, 44, 45, 58, 70, 86
Powell and Morse & Co 124. See also American Fish Guano Company
Powell brothers 124
Powellton vii, 150. See also Wachapreague
Powhatan 18
Princess Royal 122
Project Anaconda 114
Protector 146
Pungoteague v, viii, 9, 23, 31, 32, 43, 91, 103, 104, 109, 113, 115, 116, 117, 120, 126, 127, 128, 129, 160
Pungoteague Creek 9, 22, 57, 80, 82, 84, 86, 117, 124, 129, 160
Pyle, Howard 27, 28, 29, 30, 33, 41

Q

Queen of Clippers 123
Quinby iv, vii, 34, 39, 47, 102, 149, 150, 151, 152, 153
Quinby Bridge 151, 154
Quinby, Upshur 150, 151

R

railroad iii, iv, v, vii, 2, 4, 9, 10, 11, 25, 26, 27, 28, 29, 33, 51, 63, 64, 65, 82, 83, 94, 96, 104, 106, 123, 126, 127, 128, 150, 152

Ramshorn Channel 159
Raynor, George A. (Captain) 86, 93, 94
Read, George H. 92, 93
Read's Wharf 9, 88, 92, 93. See also Morley's Wharf
Reconstruction 127
Red Bank 60, 66
Red Bank Creek 22, 61, 148, 159
Red Bank Landing 79, 148
Red Bank Neck iv
Revels 24
Revels Island 26, 27
Richards, Vernon 99
Richmond Enquirer 42
Richmond, Virginia 44
Riley, John 116, 117
Rose Cottage 36, 46
Rue's Wharf 10
Rue, William J. 10
Rumsey, David 23, 24

S

Salicornia 155
salt-making 14, 54, 70, 90
saltworks 14, 54, 55, 64, 72, 90, 91
Saltworks 90, 91
Saltworks Road 54, 90
Saltworks Wharf 92, 93
Sandfordville 25
Sand Hills 24. See also Savage Neck
Sanford 25. See also Sandfordville
Savage Creek 4, 17. See also The Gulf
Savage family 19
Savage Neck vi, 3, 15, 17, 101, 131, 133, 134, 159
Savage Neck Dunes Natural Area

Preserve (NAP) 15, 131, 132, 133, 134, 135, 136
Savage Neck Road 18, 135
Savage, Thomas 13, 15, 17, 18, 19
sawmill 91, 93
Saxis iv, 8
Scarburgh, Edmund II (Colonel) 37, 38, 55, 70, 71, 72, 73, 74, 75, 76, 77, 78, 89, 90, 109, 110
Scarburgh, Mary 72, 109
Scarburgh Neck 9, 72, 128, iv
school 18, 19, 72, 88, 97, 98, 99, 101, 103, 107, 108, 126, 141, 151, 158
Scribner's Monthly 28
sea level 131, 134, 155, 156, 157
seaside vii, 1, 3, 4, 5, 6, 8, 13, 14, 20, 22, 24, 25, 33, 36, 39, 51, 64, 72, 75, 90, 102, 119, 124, 134, 138, 147, 148, 149, 151, 153, 156, 159, 160
Seaside Road iii, 149, 154
Sea View 25
Selma 43
Shadyside vi, 25, 64, 91, 127, 159
Shaw, Gayle i
Sheep's Branch 91
Shields 104, 106
Shield's Wharf 10
Ship Shoal 25
Shiras, George 26, 27
Silver Beach 10, 94, 95
Simoneaston Bay 4, 161
Simoneaston Creek 4
skiff 95, 118, 141
slavery 31, 32
slaves 31, 32, 33, 59, 63, 89, 128, 146
Sluitkill Neck 5, 8, iv
Smith, Albert 107
Smith, Frances Savage 152

Smith Island vi, 14, 15, 24, 25, 54, 156
Smith Island (Maryland) 76
Smith, Jimmy 105
Smith, John 18
Smith, Long 98
Solway Queen 123
South Bay vi
spartina 2, 6, 142, 143, 149, 154, 157
Spartina alterniflora 142
spartina patens 134
steamboat 9, 28, 29, 79, 80, 81, 82, 83, 84, 86, 87, 88, 91, 92, 93, 94, 104, 109
steamship 45, 80, 82, 85, 93, 96, 114
Sterling, Anne 105, 106, 107
Sterling, Bill i, 101, 102, 107
Stevens, Jim 116
Stevens, John 116
Stewart, John 98
Stewart, Joshua 91
St. George's Church 103, 109, 117, 129
St. James Episcopal Church 49
Stone, Thomas 38, 58, 71
Stone, William (Captain) 36, 37, 50, 58, 71
St. Paul's Church 117, 129
Stringham, Silas Horton (Captain) 114
Studies of the Virginia Eastern Shore in the Seventeenth Century 31, 58, 76
Sue 84, 85, 86, 93, 94
Sunnyside iii
Susquehanna River 148
Swans Gut Creek 3, 161
Sycamore Bend 65
Sycamore Turn 65
Sylvan Retreat 43. See also Bull Farm

T

Tangier Island 124, 146
Tanner, Henry S. 23, 24
Taplin, Guy 51, 52, 53
Tarkill Road 8
Tasley iv
Taylor Branch 9, 129
Taylor, Cornelius T. 59, 60, 120
Taylor Creek viii, 9, 117, 159, 160
Teackle Farm 104, 110, 111
Teackle Road 104
Teackles Landing vii, 150. See also Wachapreague
Teackle, Thomas (Reverend) 103, 109
Teches Island 23
Temperanceville iv
terra incognita 24, 26
Terres, John K. 137, 138
The Eastern Shore During the War of Secession Period and Reconstruction 117, 127
The Eastern Shore - Maryland and Virginia 6
The Eastern Shore News 128
The End of an Era 21
The Financial Times of London 53
The Gulf 17, 159
The Material World of Eyre Hall - Four Centuries of Chesapeake History 14
The Nature Conservancy (TNC) 102, 103, 138, 156
The Virginia Magazine of History and Biography 73
Thistle 144
Thomas Wharf 149
tierces 122, 123
tiger beetle 131, 133
tobacco 2, 8, 28, 39, 55, 56, 57, 58, 59, 73, 92
Toft, Anne 38, 70, 71, 72, 73, 74, 75, 76, 77, 78, 110
Turkey Pen Pickers 104
Turkey Pens v, 104. See also Craddockville
Turner, Bill 103
Turner, Burleigh 99
Turner, David 103
Turner, William H. (Doctor) 103
Twyford, Margaret Malana 88, 89, 90, 91, 92, 93, 94, 95, 97, 98, 99, 100
Twyford, Roland 88

U

Underhill Creek 160
Union 113, 114, 115, 118
Upper Rack (Wreck) Island 24
Upshur, Abel 36, 37
Upshur, Abel Parker (Judge) 40, 41, 44, 45, 46
Upshur, Anne Floyd 47, 49
Upshur, Ann Parker 40, 42, 44, 45
Upshur, Arthur 34, 35, 36, 37, 38, 39, 42, 50, 71
Upshur, Arthur II 39, 48
Upshur, Arthur IV 40
Upshur Bay 149, 150, 153, 160
Upshur Creek 148
Upshur, Elizabeth Brown 46
Upshur family i, 34, 35, 36, 37, 39, 40, 41, 42, 43, 44, 45, 46, 47, 48, 49, 50, 95, 101, 150
Upshur Family in Virginia 34

Upshur, George 43
Upshur, George Parker (Commander) 43
Upshur, John 35, 38, 42, 43
Upshur, John Andrews i, 34, 35
Upshur, John Brown 46
Upshur, Littleton 40, 42, 44, 45
Upshur, Littleton II (Colonel) 42, 43
Upshur, Margaret Eyre Parker 43
Upshur, Mary Elizabeth 46
Upshur, Mary Hammond Jacob 39
Upshur, Mary Risden 38, 39
Upshur Neck vii, 3, 36, 39, 45, 48, 148, 149, 150, 152, 153, iv
Upshur Neck Road 2
Upshur, Sarah Brown 39, 48
Upshur, Susan 46
Upshur, Thomas T. i
Upshur, Thomas Teackle 111
Upshur, Thomas Teackle II 48
U.S. Naval Academy 43
U.S. Navy 119
U.S. Route 13 iii, 9, 18, 69, 96, 138, 139
U.S.S. Levant 43
U.S.S. Princeton 44, 45
U.S.S. Truston 43

V

Vaucluse 40, 41, 42, 43, 44, 46
Vaucluse Shores 46. See also Vaucluse
Virginia 82
Virginia Coast Reserve 102, 156
Virginia Department of Conservation and Recreation (DCR) 131
Virginia Department of Historic Resources 18
Virginia Historical Society 49
Virginia's Eastern Shore 17, 34, 46, 77, 89, 111, 146
Virginia's Eastern Shore - A History of Northampton and Accomack Counties 49

W

Wachapreague iv, vii, 89, 148, 150, 160
Wachapreague Road 149
Wallop, John 63
Wallops 24, 59, 60
Wallops Flight Facility 4, 69
Wallops Island 63, 69, 156
Wallops Neck vii, 4, 8, 59, 63, iv
Ward, Cornelius 97
Wardtown 10, 25, 88, 89, 90, 91, 92, 97, 98, 99
Ward, Wales 91
Warehouse Creek 159
Warehouse Prong 57, 160
Warehouse Road 57
War of 1812 42, 43
warrant day 128
Warwick Plantation vii, 34, 39, 40, 45, 47, 48, 150, 160
Washington, DC 45
watermill 91
Watkinson, Cornelius 130
Wattsville vii, 161
Wellington Neck vi, 4, 64, 159
Wescoat's Point 17
Whispering Pines 48
White, Frank (Lieutenant Colonel)

179

115, 117
Whitelaw, Paula Oertel 47, 48, 49
Whitelaw, Ralph T. i, 17, 18, 34, 40, 44, 46, 47, 48, 49, 76, 77, 89, 104, 111, 128, 146, 153, 154
Whites Creek 69, 161
Whites Neck 8, iv
Wildfowl Carving and Collecting 53
Wilkins Beach 15
Wilkins Beach Hotel 16
Wilkins family 40, 46
Wilkins, Horace 99
William Bradley & Bro. 25
Williamsburg, Virginia 44
Willis Wharf 149, 154, 155
Wilmington, Delaware 27, 28, 30, 83, 85, 93
Wilsonia Neck vi, 4, 37, 50, 58, 64, 71, 159
Wilsonia Wharf 25
Winders Neck vii, 3, 8, iv
windmill 75, 91
Wise, E. Spencer 81
Wise family i
Wise, Henry A. (Governor) 21, 147
Wise, Jennings C. i, 37, 76, 111
Wise, John Sergeant i, 21, 22, 147
Wise, Sarah Cropper 147. See also Cropper, Sarah
Worcester Railroad 25, 27
World War I 47, 97
World War II iv, 15, 19, 105, 107, 125, 140

Yeardley, Francis 37
Ye Beare and Ye Cubb 127, 130
Ye Kingdome of Accawmacke 37, 76, 111
Yeo Neck viii, 9, 84, iv
York River 86

Y

Yahoo of Craddock Neck 66, 101, 103, 109, 110, 111

www.ingramcontent.com/pod-product-compliance
Lightning Source LLC
Chambersburg PA
CBHW050904160426
43194CB00011B/2283